Persuading with Data

Persuading with Data

A guide to designing, delivering, and defending your data

BY MIRO KAZAKOFF

The MIT Press

Cambridge, Massachusetts | London, England

The MIT Press would like to thank the anonymous peer reviewers who provided comments on drafts of this book. The generous work of academic experts is essential for establishing the authority and quality of our publications. We acknowledge with gratitude the contributions of these otherwise uncredited readers.

This book was set in Soleil and Adobe Caslon by Elizabeth Moran in Montague, Massachusetts. Printed and bound in the United States of America.

Design Team:
Elizabeth Moran, Art Director
Candace Hope, Producer

Library of Congress Cataloging-in-Publication Data
Names: Kazakoff, Miro, author.
Title: Persuading with data : a guide to designing, delivering, and defending your data / Miro Kazakoff.
Description: Cambridge, Massachusetts : The MIT Press, [2022] | Includes bibliographical references and index.
Identifiers: LCCN 2021014619 | ISBN 9780262543279 (paperback)
Subjects: LCSH: Business presentations—Graphic methods. | Information visualization. | Persuasion (Psychology)
Classification: LCC HF5718.22 .K395 2022 | DDC 658.4/52—dc23
LC record available at https://lccn.loc.gov/2021014619

10   9   8   7   6   5   4   3

Contents

The book is divided into four parts. The chapters within each part build on each other, but the parts can be read and taught in any order.

The parts proceed from the micro to the macro. Part I starts within your own brain and how it perceives data. Part II focuses on how to optimize an individual graph. Part III moves out to the structure and organization of an effective communication. Finally, Part IV ends with strategies to present data well and deal with the ultimate complexity: other people's responses.

PART IV

Delivering and Defending Your Data

How to prepare for and respond to your audience

Introduction

The existence of this book flows from a frustrating fact: our brains were not designed to handle the volume of data that assaults us every day. The tools and techniques presented here rest on the premise that when you communicate data effectively, you serve a greater good. By providing others with a clearer understanding of our world, you free your audience to focus their mental energy on the hard work of making good decisions.

Our brains, however, provide plenty of obstacles on the path from raw data to good decisions. This book exists to help you see those obstacles more clearly, dodge them more gracefully, and lead others to better choices.

Who this book is for

Persuading with Data is for business students and professionals like you who explain analytical results to others, especially audiences who are less sophisticated about the topic than you are. Those audiences may be executives or managers within your organization, customers, external stakeholders, or other groups who act based on the analyses you perform. This book will improve your ability to visualize data so that it is clear to others, arm you with the tools to organize those visuals into compelling and logical communications, and increase your ability to help audiences accept and act on the data.

What makes this book different

This book provides an overview of the entire data communication process, from designing effective graphs, to organizing your data into clear structures, to delivering your data to an audience and defending your results. Unlike most books that focus on just one of those topics, this one synthesizes a wide variety of skills needed by modern data professionals. It goes beyond the best practices of data visualization to present the entire toolkit needed to create effective business communications. Unlike many other books on these topics, *Persuading with Data*:

1. Addresses both explanatory visualization and communication strategy

Most data visualization books focus exclusively on creating good graphs. This book brings the focus back to how you can use those visuals to create effective communications that persuade others to take actions informed by the data. It will equip you with the frameworks and principles to structure your thinking clearly, identify the implications that emerge, design effective data visualizations, deliver your visualizations to an audience, and defend your results. It can serve as a primer on both explanatory visualization and strategic communication.

2. Integrates both a practical and academic perspective

This book emerges from a combination of analytical, practical, and academic experience. Combining my academic and practical experience, I created the MIT Sloan's "Communicating with Data" classes. Prior to that, I studied both English and computer science before spending over a decade in the technology industry communicating technical information to nontechnical audiences at companies like WPP (the media holding company), Bain & Company, and Hubspot. I've seen the tools in this book work in both the classroom and the workplace.

3. Supports readers with different backgrounds

The content has been tested across a wide variety of formats and audiences, including academic classes and workplace trainings with undergraduates, recent graduates, early career, mid-career, and executive-level professionals. It is appropriate for readers with no prior background beyond an introductory business education or general work experience, while still being useful for those with decades of experience. The frameworks and concepts have been refined for clarity and efficacy based on extensive feedback. They are reliably useful and accessible to a broad range of business professionals.

4. Incorporates real-world examples

The book incorporates real-world examples drawn from hundreds of professionals and tested with audiences ranging from undergraduates to working professionals. The examples span a variety of industries, organizations, and disciplines and show how the frameworks in this book apply to a wide variety of audiences.

5. Includes supplemental teaching materials

The supplemental lesson plans, slides, and answer keys and grading rubrics associated with the text allow for the turnkey creation of an entire college-level class. The support material has been used to train multiple faculty members with limited background in data visualization to deliver high-quality student experiences. Each chapter includes an exercise that encourages readers to apply what they have learned. Additional exercises that require students to go from raw data to complete communication are available via the MIT Press for teachers who assign all or part of the book to their students.

How this book is organized

The book is divided into four parts. The chapters within each part build on each other, but the parts can be read and taught in any order.

The parts proceed from the micro to the macro. Part I starts within your own brain and how it perceives data. Part II focuses on how to optimize an individual graph. Part III moves out to the structure and organization of an effective communication. Finally, Part IV ends with strategies to present data well and deal with the ultimate complexity: other people's responses.

PART I
Understanding Perception: How and why graphs work

Chapter 1: Know Your Own Mind (in order to change others')

Communication is a process of encoding ideas into words, pictures, and sounds that can be decoded by others. This chapter illuminates the key challenges the human brain faces in that process. It explains why communicating data to others introduces a different set of challenges from those confronted when analyzing data. The rest of this book explores the implications of these challenges and how they inform the best practices and frameworks you will use to combat them.

Chapter 2: See How Graphs Work (inside your brain)

Graphs are a critical tool in communicating data. They allow audiences to see relationships that would be too complex or even impossible to convey through numerals. Even the most complex graphs take advantage of a few features of our visual perception system. This chapter explains how audiences decode graphical information. The first section covers basic features of visual perception. The second section addresses the preattentive attributes and Gestalt principles that inform effective design. Mastering these concepts will allow you to create graphs that audiences can decode easily and reliably. The exercise at the end of the chapter will help hone your ability to see how the sections function together by challenging you to break down a graph into its components.

PART II
Designing Your Data: How to design effective graphs and slides

Chapter 3: Choose the Right Graph (for your data)

Graphs take advantage of our ability to see relationships. So, selecting the best graph starts with understanding the data relationship you want to highlight. This chapter introduces the major types of relationships and then provides a deeper dive into the best practices and most common graph types used to show those relationships. At the end of the chapter, test your ability to recognize data relationships by categorizing and sketching graphs based on the relationship they ought to show.

Chapter 4: Simplify to Amplify (your message)

Even thoughtfully built graphs fail to persuade audiences when they are burdened by needless clutter and excess complexity. The goal is not to reduce the complexity of the data your graph visualizes. The goal is to create graphs that are perfectly transparent windows into the underlying data. This chapter presents two approaches to simplifying your graphs and amplifying your message: maximizing the data–ink ratio and creating an information hierarchy. The exercise tests your ability to amplify the data by reducing clutter.

Chapter 5: Build Effective Slides (with the point in mind)

Most business audiences consume graphs within slide presentations. This chapter moves from building effective graphs to the process of building effective slides that present those graphs to others. It focuses on the most important part of slide design: identifying the point of each slide. The chapter walks through how to write the point as the headline of your slide and a series of tests to help reinforce effective design choices. The exercise allows you to practice creating graphs that reinforce the slide's headline.

PART III
Organizing Your Data: How to arrange data into compelling communications

Chapter 6: Structure Your Data (so others can follow it)

Clear communications build on clear, logical foundations. Part III shifts our focus from creating effective data visualizations to the skills required to assemble those visuals into compelling communications. This chapter introduces the Minto pyramid as a tool to organize your thoughts. It shows how to structure your thinking with a pyramid outline in order to strengthen the clarity of your communications, how to use a story to identify your main idea, and how to test the logical rigor of your arguments. The final section demonstrates how a Minto pyramid easily converts into a wide variety of communications. The exercise challenges you to structure a compelling argument based on a business case and the needs of your audience.

Chapter 7: Frame the Data to Persuade (so the audience acts)

This chapter introduces the factors that influence your audience beyond the quality of your analysis and the clarity of your structure. It discusses how the audience's prior knowledge and biases should influence your approach. The Elaboration Likelihood Model provides a framework for understanding how non-data factors inform the audience's decision-making process, and the remainder of the chapter presents strategies to maximize the impact of your communication by explaining What's In It For Them—the WIIFT—and framing your points around common thinking patterns. The exercise challenges you to create Minto pyramids designed for specific audiences.

PART IV
Delivering and Defending Your Data: How to prepare for and respond to your audience

Chapter 8: Present Your Data (with less preparation)

Despite the common expression, data does not speak for itself. Data can't talk, and it certainly can't explain its implications for your business. This chapter explains how to give your data a voice in front of an audience. The first half of the chapter outlines the TOP-T framework, an approach to presenting data-oriented slides. Mastering this framework will help you clarify the meaning of the data, accelerate your audience's understanding, and increase your persuasive power. The second half of the chapter goes into advanced presentation techniques. The exercise provides practice slides to help you sharpen your skills.

Chapter 9: Prepare for Resistance (because resistance shows they care)

Eventually, every communicator meets with resistance from their audience. This chapter explains how to anticipate the kinds of challenges you are likely to encounter and how to prepare for them. It explains how understanding the nature of change can help predict your audience's behavior, and it introduces the Audience Confusion Matrix so that you can prepare an appropriate response. The final section of the chapter provides some strategies for defusing difficult situations. The exercise offers a chance to predict the audience response to different scenarios and think through the appropriate preparation.

Part I

Understanding Perception

—

How and why graphs work

CHAPTER 1

Know Your Own Mind

(in order to change others')

———

Source: https://xkcd.com/523

Communication is a process of encoding ideas into words, pictures, and sounds that can be decoded by others. This chapter illuminates the key challenges the human brain faces in that process. It explains why communicating data to others introduces a different set of challenges from those confronted when analyzing data. The rest of this book explores the implications of these challenges and how they inform the best practices and frameworks you will use to combat them.

Understand the challenges of communicating data

If communicating data were easier, the world would be full of better decisions. You have undoubtedly even seen people you respect make decisions that seemed to be informed by bad data or misinformed by sound data. Perhaps you've wondered, "Why is everyone so incompetent?"—a thought you likely followed up with, "Except me, of course."

This book can't answer the question of whether you are surrounded by idiots, but it can definitively state that you are surrounded by humans. And humans, it turns out, face certain challenges that are central to the communication process itself.

Fundamentally, communication is a process of encoding, transmitting, and decoding information. We encode the ideas in our minds as sounds, images, and words in order to transmit them to others. Decoding is the reverse process that takes place in someone else's mind, where sounds, images, and words get decoded back into the ideas they were meant to represent. In between, we have two primary transmission channels at our disposal:[1]

 Visual: We can encode information visually in pictures, graphs, or the words you are reading right now. These encodings eventually travel as light waves to the eyes of your audience.

 Auditory: We can encode information in sounds, such as speech. These encodings eventually travel through the air as sound waves where they are received by the ears of your audience.

This process of encoding, transmitting, and decoding is communication. It is also the source of all communication problems. Three key challenges complicate our attempts to communicate data.

Challenge	What it means	What it implies
The challenge of multiple minds	Different minds decode the same encoding differently.	That which is clear to you is not necessarily clear to others.
The Curse of Knowledge	We forget what it was like before we knew what we now know.	
The burden of cognitive load	Our brains minimize effortful processing whenever possible.	Explaining data to others is a distinct mindset and skill set.

---

[1] Every sense organ represents a potential communication channel, but taste, touch, and smell are discouraged as workplace communication channels. Just ask anyone downwind of the coworker who likes to microwave fish for lunch.

Challenge 1: The challenge of multiple minds

Try an exercise using the set of symbols on this page to illustrate the challenges of encoding and decoding. As you glance at each symbol, notice how your brain immediately decodes each symbol. Notice that other encodings may occur to you, too. Focus on that first thought. This process of watching your own thinking is called *metacognition*. It's a critical skill for learning to understand the decoding process, and it is one you will develop throughout this book. As you process each encoding, write down what first came to your mind.

Encoding	When you saw this encoding, you thought of . . .
II	
2	
=	
10	

Look at each of the encodings in the table. Jot down what you decoded each one as. Notice your immediate response and write that down. Notice which ones you were able to decode more quickly and which took longer.

What first popped into your head when you saw II? Many people see a pause sign, parallel lines, the numeral eleven, the roman numeral two, or eyes on a face. Some struggle to see anything meaningful.

What about 2? Almost everyone reports this as the number two. Technically, it is the Arabic numeral two, a very specific squiggle that we all learned to decode as the number two. Remember that it's only by common agreement that this squiggle encodes a concept that we will call "two-ness."

The numeral two is such a universal encoding that most people jump from the encoding to the underlying concept in an instant. It happens so quickly that the encoding feels like the concept itself, but the idea of two-ness is different from the encoding we use to represent it. Separating the concept from the way it is encoded in your own mind is an important skill to develop in order to make wise data-visualization choices.

Did you decode = quickly or slowly? Those literate in Chinese will decode this encoding to the number two and will do so as fast as almost everyone decodes the Arabic numeral two to the same idea. This encoding, which is perfectly clear to over a billion people, is gibberish to those unfamiliar with it.

How about 10? Most recognize a familiar pattern quickly and decode this to the number ten, but it's also the number two encoded using binary. All that separates this encoding from representing ten or two is the context.

The point of this exercise is to illustrate the complexity of encoding and decoding even simple ideas. Every single one of these encodings is a way of representing the concept of two-ness, but a variety of factors influenced how your specific mind decoded each one.

This is the fundamental challenge of communicating anything, including data: one brain encodes information with a clear intention, but multiple brains decode it. How we decode hinges on a variety of factors. To communicate effectively, you need to understand these factors and cultivate a sensitivity to the differing needs of every audience. If you want many minds to reliably decode data in the way you intend them to, you need to design, structure, and deliver data starting with the assumption that the audience's minds do not necessarily match your own.

MANY FACTORS INFLUENCE DECODING

Factor	Example
Context	Ordering: When the Arabic numeral 2 comes first, audiences are more likely to decode the other encodings as 2.
Prior experience	Language: Those familiar with a language will be able to decode it (e.g., English, Chinese, Python).
Familiarity	Acronyms: Depending on your familiarity with programming or pricing, ASP may mean Application Service Provider or Average Selling Price to you.
Culture	Color use: The color red is used to encode losses in Western cultures and gains in some Eastern cultures.
Channel	Font size: A perfectly readable font on a printout may be unintelligible when projected in an auditorium.
Biology	Colorblindness: About 4.5% of the population has some kind of color vision deficiency (CVD) that makes it difficult to discriminate between different sets of colors.[2]
Communicator	Accents: Nonnative speakers may struggle with communicators who have strong accents from a different language.

---

[2] The population average distorts the distribution. Almost everyone with a color vision deficiency is male. It affects about 1 in 12 men and 1 in 200 women.

Challenge 2: The Curse of Knowledge

Our minds have a few curious traits. When a new idea shows up, it's evaluated with stunning speed. If the idea looks familiar, and nothing suggests a need for further inspection, we tend to accept it and incorporate it into our understanding of the world. Once it's accepted, an even more curious thing happens: we forget what life was like before that idea came along. This ancient hex is the Curse of Knowledge:[3] the phenomenon that when you learn something, you forget what it was like not to know it. You can even forget that the information was ever new to you.

As an example, notice what happens when you look at the image below. What does your brain resolve the image to? How quickly does that happen?

Source: coolbubble.com

This is a complex image. There are many more elements and colors here than in a complicated data visualization, but your brain probably decoded it as a rose with just a casual glance.

But did you see the dolphin?

Go back and look a second time. Now that you've been primed to look for it, it's more likely you'll see it (if not, check the next page).

Once you see the dolphin, it's impossible to un-see it. That is the Curse of Knowledge. Our brains will not allow us to return to the state we were in before we learned what we know now.

The Curse of Knowledge is well documented. It happens as soon as we learn something. Not only does it cause us to forget what it was like not to know something, we tend to forget that the information was ever new to us. The more you know, the stronger the curse gets. Experts tend to suffer its effects more than novices.

Unwinding the Curse of Knowledge is one of the primary challenges of communicating data. Building even the simplest graph requires you to spend orders of magnitude more time with the data than your audience. Let's say your audience spends five to ten

---

[3] Check out Chip and Dan Heath's excellent book *Made to Stick* for a deep dive into the Curse of Knowledge. I'm adopting their convention of capitalizing it to "give it the drama we think it deserves."

seconds decoding your graph. Even the speediest of Excel wizards would struggle to create, format, clean, label, and copy a graph into PowerPoint in under 100 seconds. That's already 10× the time your audience has spent thinking about this information. Effective communication must constantly fight the tendency of our own brains to forget what it's like for an audience who doesn't know what we know.

Challenge 3: The burden of cognitive load

Our brains like ease. They dislike strain. As soon as our brains think we understand something, we tend to stop looking deeper. In the dolphin and rose example, once you saw the rose, you probably stopped looking for any other shapes encoded in the image. Why wouldn't you?

Here's another example. What pops into your head as you look at the encoding below?

$$17^2$$

Most people see this image and think "seventeen squared." If you had to memorize the square root of every number up to 20 in elementary school you might have immediately seen 289, but most people stop once they recognize the symbol and don't do the math it implies.

That is because multiplying out 17 by 17 is a cognitively taxing process. It puts load on our brain. As humans, we try to avoid that cognitive load and conserve mental energy whenever possible. This effect is so strong that we are more likely to believe statements that take less cognitive load to process. Take the following two pieces of data:[4]

The first pie chart was published in 1794.

The first pie chart was published in 1803.

---

[4] This example and this section are adapted from Nobel Laureate Daniel Kahneman's summary of all the ways in which our minds fail us: *Thinking, Fast and Slow*. Much of this book can be read as an exploration of the ways in which an aversion to cognitive load shapes our interpretation of the world.

Neither is true. William Playfair published the first pie chart in 1801, but when these two statements are shown to a large number of people, more people are inclined to believe the first one because the bold type makes it more legible. The increased readability of the first statement puts less cognitive load on our brains. We are more likely to believe what is easier to absorb.

The first design implication of this principle is that your data must be legible to be believable. As a result, there is no arbitrary "correct" font size for a presentation. The optimal size depends on your audience and the channel through which you are communicating. That means using a larger font for presentations delivered in an auditorium than when the audience is reading a printout.

A more general implication is that communicating data isn't about dumbing down your ideas. It's about stripping away anything that could get in the way of audience understanding. It's about using design to maximize the signal of your ideas and reduce extraneous noise. Or as Albert Einstein is rumored to have said: "Make it as simple as possible, but no simpler."[5]

The best practices laid out in the rest of this book arise in response to these three core challenges of communication: the challenge of many minds, the Curse of Knowledge, and the burden of cognitive load. Without them, persuading others would be easy. Every other mind would see things the same way we do. It would be easy to remember exactly which new ideas shifted our thinking, and audiences would have infinite capacity to bear the cognitive load of absorbing information at any level of detail. Alas, they do not.

---

[5] While the simplified version of this quote was conveyed to the *New York Times* by the composer Roger Sessions, the closest documented version of this concept that can be directly attributed to Einstein is even more applicable to data analysts: "It can scarcely be denied that the supreme goal of all theory is to make the irreducible basic elements as simple and as few as possible without having to surrender the adequate representation of a single datum of experience." May we all strive to meet this standard.

Garson O'Toole, "Everything Should Be Made as Simple as Possible, But Not Simpler," *QuoteInvestigator.com*, last modified May 13, 2011, https://quoteinvestigator.com/2011/05/13/einstein-simple/.

Shift your mindset to explain data to others

These three challenges lie dormant while you conduct your analysis. They only present themselves when you begin the communication process. There's no need to worry about multiple minds until you need to communicate with them. The Curse of Knowledge doesn't emerge until you have learned something from the analysis, and the burden of cognitive load falls on those you are asking to decode your analysis. Addressing these three challenges requires you to adopt a different mindset and employ a different skill set to communicate data from the one you developed to analyze the data itself.

The process of figuring out what the data means is so different from the process of explaining those results to others that these two phases of data analysis have different names: the exploring data phase and the explaining data phase. The different names highlight the different skills and mindsets needed to do each one effectively.

	The exploring data phase "the answer stage"	The explaining data phase "the telling others stage"
Intended audience	Yourself	Someone else
Desired complexity	High (Show all possible options)	Low (Focus on the answer)
Goal	Understand what the data means	Explain the meaning of the data to others
Use	The answer is the output of your work	The answer is an input to someone else's decisions

The exploring data phase is what Chip and Dan Heath call "the answer stage." This is the part of the process most people think of when working with data. It is the focus of most data analysis classes: exploring and visualizing data in order to understand what the data means, what questions we ought to ask of it, and what answers it might provide. Exploring data is an iterative process. Varying your analytical approach might open up new perspectives and often shifts the underlying question. Exploring is the process of sifting through data, like panning for gold, to find the nuggets worthy of others' attention.[6]

This book assumes your work and other classes have trained you well on the exploring data phase. This book focuses entirely on the explaining data phase, or what the Heath brothers call "the telling others stage." This is the stage where you pick out the nuggets

---

[6] This example is rather nakedly derived from Cole Nussbaumer Knaflic's oysters and pearls metaphor, an illustration so apt it's reliably adopted by almost everyone who reads it in her excellent book *Storytelling with Data*.

and polish them so that others can easily recognize the gold you found. A separate approach is needed because the mindset that served you well in the exploratory "answer" stage can undermine you in the explanatory "telling others" stage.

For example, high-complexity visualizations are more efficient in the exploratory stage. The more complex the data visualization, the more aspects of the data that can be evaluated simultaneously, the more rapidly the question can be refined, and the faster the answer can be found.

In the explanatory phase, complexity is the enemy. Your audience needs to see the key insights quickly and clearly. Excess complexity confuses audiences, distracts from your point, and risks introducing noise that suggests the wrong interpretation.

But introducing a new stage of work, converting your analysis into a communication, shifts the workload around. It moves work that used to go into convincing others and correcting their misinterpretations into work that happens before you even communicate with them.

To avoid the difficult mental work of the explanatory phase, some communicators simply narrate the audience through their exploratory process, sharing every step and visual they used to reach their conclusion. For the communicator, the journey may be a heroic tale of conquering ignorance through ingenuity and perseverance. Audiences are less generous in their assessment. Spare them the burden of reliving the exploratory process, and create communications that serve their needs. Take them right to the gold, not on a tour of all the places you came up empty-handed.

Treat the explanatory phase of your analysis as a completely different mental process, and trust that the clarity of your explanation will give your work the credibility it needs to persuade others. The chapters that follow provide the road map to get you there.

Key concepts from this chapter

Explaining data to others is a separate phase from the data analysis phase. It requires both a different mindset and different data visualizations.

THE EXPLAINING DATA TO OTHERS CHECKLIST

Have you accounted for	Remember to ask yourself
Multiple minds	• Do you understand the background and context of your audience? • Do you know what type of analysis they typically consume and how often?
The Curse of Knowledge	• Have you explained your analysis to someone else? • Have you explained your analysis to someone with the same knowledge level your audience will have?
Cognitive load	• Have you removed any complexity that isn't required to understand your findings? • Have you focused on the results of your analysis rather than the process you used to get there?

If you remember nothing else . . .

Communication is a process of encoding, transmitting, and decoding information. This process is also the source of all communication problems.

You cannot unsee the dolphin.

Communicating data isn't about dumbing down your ideas. It's about stripping away everything that could get in the way of audience understanding.

Take your audience right to the gold, not on a tour of all the places you came up empty-handed.

CHAPTER 2

See How Graphs Work
(inside your brain)

—

Source: https://xkcd.com/833

Graphs are a critical tool in communicating data. They allow audiences to see relationships that would be too complex or even impossible to convey through numerals. Even the most complex graphs take advantage of a few features of our visual perception system. This chapter explains how audiences decode graphical information. The first section covers basic features of visual perception. The second section addresses the preattentive attributes and Gestalt principles that inform effective design. Mastering these concepts will allow you to create graphs that audiences can decode easily and reliably. The exercise at the end of the chapter will help you hone your ability to see how the sections function together by challenging you to break down a graph into its components.

How we decode graphs

The impact of graphs comes from the visual processing system's powerful ability to see relationships between visual elements. Look around. Notice how quickly and easily you are able to determine the size and relative distance of every object in your field of vision. This is because of the human ability to process the visual relationships between the size and position of everything you see. Your brain just built a coherent three-dimensional map of your environment with no perceptible cognitive load.

Part of how your brain filters all this visual information into a coherent picture is by grouping information into chunks. If you close your eyes, you probably can't remember a complete picture of everything you just saw. Instead, your brain remembers chunks of information: a cluttered desk, trees through a window, a bookshelf. Effective graphs similarly group information into logical chunks to lower cognitive load on the audience.

The brain also filters by focusing on things that are prominent or different. This visual quality is called *salience*. Salient visual elements are the things that stick out. Our brains are wired to see the one moving tree—that might have a bear behind it—among the hundreds of trees along a forest walk. Isolated movement is highly salient. Salience is an example of how our brains limit cognitive load. Only one visual element can be most salient at a time.

Graphs take advantage of these principles by encoding quantitative information visually and displaying it in relation to one or more axes.[1] Nearly instantly, our brain recognizes the visual relationships between elements on the graph, groups information into chunks, and identifies the most salient elements. Since this process happens so quickly, understanding how each of these concepts manifests when an audience looks at a graph is a critical step toward building more effective communications.

We see the relationships

Graphs tap into our superpower to quickly and easily see visual relationships. The statistician Francis Anscombe generated the data set that follows to illustrate the capacity of our visual system (as well as the profound impact of outliers on data sets).

---

[1] More precisely, graphs display information in relation to one or more axes that help decode the values and scale of the visual elements. Graphs in this text refer specifically to this type of visual encoding. When needed, "charts" will be used as the broader term, encompassing graphs, tables, diagrams, and other information displays that use position and images to encode meaning beyond text. Though this is the technical distinction, the term "chart" and "graph" are used interchangeably in everyday use.

	Group A		Group B		Group C		Group D	
	x	y	x	y	x	y	x	y
	10	8.04	10	9.14	10	7.46	8	6.58
	8	6.95	8	8.14	8	6.77	8	5.76
	13	7.58	13	8.74	13	12.74	8	7.71
	9	8.81	9	8.77	9	7.11	8	8.84
	11	8.33	11	9.26	11	7.81	8	8.47
	14	9.96	14	8.1	14	8.84	8	7.04
	6	7.24	6	6.13	6	6.08	8	5.25
	4	4.26	4	3.1	4	5.39	19	12.5
	12	10.84	12	9.13	12	8.15	8	5.56
	7	4.82	7	7.26	7	6.42	8	7.91
	5	5.68	5	4.74	5	5.73	8	6.89
N	11	11	11	11	11	11	11	11
mean	9.0	7.5	9.0	7.5	9.0	7.5	9.0	7.5
SD	3.2	1.9	3.2	1.9	3.2	1.9	3.2	1.9
R^2	0.82		0.82		0.82		0.82	

Source: F. J. Anscombe, "Graphs in Statistical Analysis," *American Statistician* 27 (Feb. 1973): 17–21.

The four sets are nearly statistically identical. Each column has the same mean, standard deviation, and number of elements. The correlation between the x and y for each group is the same (to two decimal places). Looking over the table, it's clear that the sets are different, but few people could quickly generate a succinct description of the differences.

Check out the graphical representation of each set below. The graphs demonstrate the relationships between each of the four sets with more clarity and speed than the table does. Anscombe used this example to argue that visualization is a critical step in data exploration. He wanted to challenge the idea that "numerical calculations are exact, but graphs are rough." His example reminds us that the purpose of graphing data is to show relationships. If we aren't demonstrating a relationship, a graph isn't a useful tool. If we are demonstrating one, a graph is likely to be faster and easier for an audience to process than a table of numbers.[2]

GRAPHS SHOW RELATIONSHIPS QUICKLY

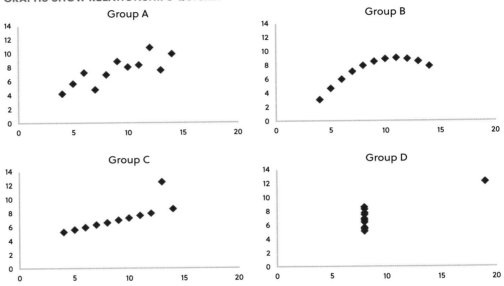

Source: F. J. Anscombe, "Graphs in Statistical Analysis," *American Statistician* 27 (Feb. 1973): 17–21.

We see the data in chunks

Our brain divides incoming information into chunks.[3] These chunks can be any grouping of concepts or symbols. What makes something a chunk is our ability to identify it as a single concept. Graphing explanatory data well is about choosing how to chunk the data.

---

[2] This is not to suggest that well-formatted tables don't have an important place in communicating data. Graphs are better at showing the relationship between values, but they aren't as good as tables at showing the specific values. Use tables when the specific values are an important factor in the decision, not just their relationship with each other.

[3] Yes, this is the technical term for this idea, though other terms like *concept* and *schema* are sometimes used to denote higher levels of abstraction.

The boundary of what counts as a chunk is flexible. Almost any set of ideas or images can be stored in a single chunk depending on how we mentally segment it. However, the limitation on how many chunks we can actively work with at the same time is strict. We generally have space for three to four chunks at a time.[4]

Graphs allow you to combine a large number of data points into a single visual chunk for easier recall. In the following table, most people treat each number as its own chunk. Perhaps they have room to remember the four most extreme numbers, which are highlighted.

SERVICE REQUESTS (PRIOR YEAR)

	Jan	Feb	Mar	Apr	May	Jun	Jul	Aug	Sep	Oct	Nov	Dec	
Machine Type A	2,751	3,850	3,260	3,521	2,420	4,071	4,214	4,027	4,401	4,763	5,006	5,611	Each number is a separate chunk.
Machine Type B	1,002	1,012	1,701	1,747	1,794	1,270	1,108	918	1,234	1,612	1,747	1,981	

A line graph groups these twenty-four numbers into two chunks: the Machine Type A line and the Machine Type B line. By creating these chunks, the pattern of each region and the relationship between them is easier to recognize and remember. Visualizing data is about chunking it in ways that make the key relationships easier to see.

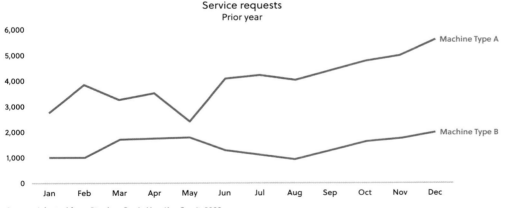

Service requests
Prior year

Machine Type A is one chunk of information.

Machine Type B is a second chunk.

Source: Adapted from Stephen Few's *Now You See it,* 2009

[4] Measuring this idea has proven tricky. Human minds vary. It's tough to experimentally re-create the havoc that is a normal person's day, and the ability to efficiently organize chunks into greater and greater levels of abstraction improves with practice. One of the hallmarks of mastery is the ability to organize information about that domain into coherent chunks. Suffice it to say, the audience has room for a lot fewer concepts on a topic than the communicator does. For more detailed discussions of memory, consult Colin Ware's *Information Visualization: Perception for Design,* as well as G. A. Miller, "The Magical Number Seven, Plus or Minus Two: Some Limits on Our Capacity for Processing Information," *Psychological Review* 63, no. 2 (1956): 81–97; and Nelson Cowan, "The Magical Number 4 in Short-Term Memory: A Reconsideration of Mental Storage Capacity," *Behavioral and Brain Sciences* 24, no. 1 (2001): 87–114.

We see the most salient elements

Our ability to filter out information is as powerful as our ability to see relationships. Our mind doesn't weigh every bit of light hitting our eyes equally. It focuses us on what is salient—what stands out. If nothing stands out, the audience may not be able to focus on the key relationships and understand what they mean. Understand salience to make sure you focus your audience in the right place, and make sure every explanatory visual has a single, most salient point.

Consider this block of numerals where everything is equally visually salient. Notice how long it takes you to count the number of sixes in the block.

Try to count the 6s.

8	4	0	2	7	6	8
3	2	5	1	2	4	0
0	7	9	6	7	2	0
5	3	7	0	5	1	8
7	6	1	1	1	4	9
8	2	2	9	7	3	3
1	8	2	7	3	6	9

There are four sixes, but it probably took you a few seconds to hunt all of them down. Now try it again in the same block of numerals, this time with exactly two changes to increase the salience of the sixes.

Now the 6s are much more salient.

8	4	0	2	7	**6**	8
3	2	5	1	2	4	0
0	7	9	**6**	7	2	0
5	3	7	0	5	1	8
7	**6**	1	1	1	4	9
8	2	2	9	7	3	3
1	8	2	7	3	**6**	9

Most people find it's much faster to count the sixes in the second block, even though the ordering is unchanged. That's because the sixes are much more visually salient than the surrounding numbers. They are a different color than the surrounding numbers and in bold. The surrounding numbers are a light gray that doesn't contrast with the page as much as the black ink in the original version. These effects increase the salience of the sixes. Our eyes gravitate to what is salient because it requires less cognitive load to find and recognize visually salient elements. Notice how the effect is erased when multiple numbers are highlighted. Nothing is salient anymore.

8	4	**0**	2	7	**6**	**8**
3	2	5	1	2	4	**0**
0	7	**9**	**6**	7	2	**0**
5	3	7	**0**	5	1	**8**
7	**6**	1	1	1	4	9
8	2	2	**9**	7	3	3
1	**8**	2	7	3	**6**	9

When multiple things try to be the focus, nothing is.

Source: Adapted from Cole Nussbaumer Knaflic's *Storytelling with Data*, 2015.

Trying to foreground multiple elements increases the cognitive load on the audience and reduces their ability to focus on any individual element. When we try to make everything salient, it turns everything into noise. The Curse of Knowledge can blind communicators to this effect. When you already know what to look for, the key elements look salient to you even when they are not salient to your audience.

We cannot control other people's eyeballs, but we can influence which elements are more salient and more likely to draw focus. Effective data communicators make deliberate choices about salience in order to fight the challenge of multiple minds. They point the audience toward meaningful patterns and away from noise. To do so, they think carefully and critically about how their graphs encode data.

How graphs encode data

Effective graphs take advantage of humans' visual processing systems by showing relationships, consolidating data points into a small number of chunks, and focusing the audience on one chunk at a time by making that chunk visually salient.

Before any of this abstraction occurs, the brain has to create meaning out of what the eye sees. This process happens so fast that it is complete before the audience even turns its conscious attention to the graph. It's called preattentive processing.[5] Effective graphs allow audiences to process complex information quickly and with low cognitive load because they take advantage of attributes we recognize in this preattentive processing stage. Another set of principles, the Gestalt principles, speak to how the brain groups visual elements.

Preattentive attributes and Gestalt principles explain why graphs work. Mastering their implications will help you make visual choices that audiences can decode more quickly and reliably.

Graphs encode data using preattentive attributes

Preattentive attributes are the grammar of data visualizations. Graphs take data and encode it visually using these attributes. For example, bar graphs encode values using the preattentive attribute of size. The taller the bar, the larger the value it encodes. Common graphs take advantage of four preattentive attributes that we recognize immediately.[6]

PREATTENTIVE ATTRIBUTES

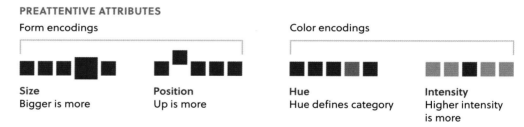

Form encodings

Size
Bigger is more

Position
Up is more

Color encodings

Hue
Hue defines category

Intensity
Higher intensity
is more

---

[5] More precisely, visual input passes through a filter called iconic memory, which chunks up information before moving select chunks into working memory. Preattentive processing happens in this iconic memory stage. Even this highly simplified explanation fails to do justice to the miraculous complexity of our eyes and brains.

[6] I've pared down the full list of preattentive attributes to focus on the core attributes used for most common graphs. Some additional preattentive attributes that can be encoded in static images are shape, curvature, blur, added marks, convex/concave shading, and stereoscopic depth. This text focuses on static graphs, which do not move or change form. In dynamic graphs, where the image is animated, motion itself is a preattentive attribute along with the subattributes of flicker and direction.

Size

Size's natural-world analogues make it the most intuitive encoding. The height, width, and volume of a tree encode its age. The bigger the tree, the older it is likely to be.

Of the three, height tends to be the easiest for us to estimate visually, followed by width. Differences in area are tricky for audiences to estimate accurately beyond identifying which areas are substantially bigger than others.

Size is the most common visual encoding. It can encode any numerical value via height, width, or area.

THREE FORMS OF SIZE ENCODING

Height   Width   Area

BEST PRACTICES FOR USING SIZE AS AN ENCODING
Always start the y-axis from zero when encoding bars
One of the few rules in visualization without notable exception is to always start the y-axis from zero when encoding with bars. Starting the y-axis from a nonzero value is called y-axis truncation. It's commonly used to distort data. Our preattentive ability to estimate height differences is so strong that audiences tend to do it automatically, even when the truncation is well marked.

Y-AXIS TRUNCATION DISTORTS DATA; START BARS FROM ZERO

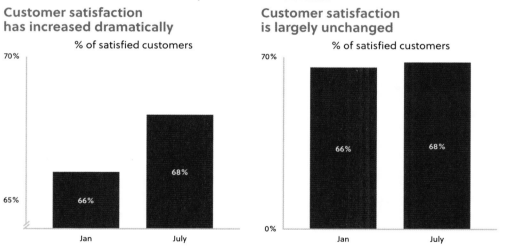

(Left) 2% difference appears to be almost double.

(Right) A more accurate graph shows the actual difference is minimal.

In the first graph, y-axis truncation and a misleading headline reinforce the incorrect initial impression that customer satisfaction scores almost doubled from January to July. The true increase is closer to 2%, but we tend to immediately assume that the visual difference in the height of the bars reflects the difference in the underlying data.

Sometimes, however, small differences are meaningful. For an internet service provider, a decline from 99.9% uptime to 99.5% might represent a significant threat to the business. If small differences are meaningful, consider graphing the inverse statistic—like downtime—to emphasize the magnitude of the change, or forgo the bar graph for other graph forms where the audience is less likely to assume a zero baseline by default.

GRAPH THE INVERSE TO AVOID Y-AXIS TRUNCATION

Average monthly downtime
Inverse of uptime

	Jan	Feb	March	April	May	June
	0.05%	0.05%	0.04%	0.05%	0.04%	0.45%

Average monthly uptime

	Jan	Feb	March	April	May	June
	99.95%	99.95%	99.96%	99.95%	99.96%	99.55%

USE ALTERNATE FORMS TO MAKE APPROPRIATE TRUNCATION CLEARER

Average monthly uptime

	Jan	Feb	March	April	May	June
	99.95%	99.95%	99.96%	99.95%	99.96%	99.55%

(Left) The inverse measure (downtime) emphasizes the scale of the change.

(Right) The audience is less likely to assume this graph starts from zero.

Position

Line graphs and scatterplots are the most common use of position as an encoding. Values can be encoded by vertical position, horizonal position, or both in the case of scatterplots. In general, a higher vertical position encodes a larger value.

THREE FORMS OF POSITION ENCODING

Points   Lines   Boxes

BEST PRACTICES FOR USING POSITION AS AN ENCODING
Remember that audiences assume up is good
Up usually encodes higher values, and higher values are better for essential business metrics like revenue, profits, and customers. As a result, audiences tend to assume that up is good and down is bad.

Unless an audience sees a metric all the time, assume they will interpret up as good until they are fully oriented to the data. Try to conform to this convention whenever possible to reduce cognitive load on the audience. When up is bad, such as the cost to acquire a new customer, add explicit notation to signal that this data is different.

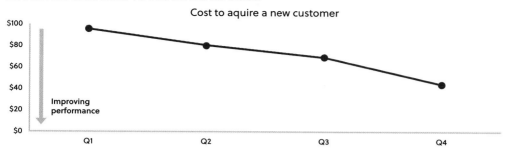

Color

There are two different preattentive forms of color used to encode meaning in graphs: hue and intensity.[7] Hue is the more precise term for what we casually refer to as color. Unlike the other preattentive attributes, hue is best used to encode categories and groups rather than different numerical values.

The other aspect of color—intensity—can be used to encode both values and categories.[8] The intensity of a color can be thought of as the opacity of the color, since that's the control that most easily adjusts it in the most common visualization programs. At zero intensity, a color would appear the same as the background.

A common hue encoding is to color stock price increases in green and stock price decreases in red. A common intensity encoding is to map water depth with different intensities of blue. Darker blue means deeper water.

---

[7] Color theory can and does fill multiple thoughtful volumes. I've picked out a few key concepts that emphasize how color can be used to lower cognitive load. In addition to multiple tools online, check out Stephen Few's *Show Me the Numbers* for a solid technical overview of color and Nancy Duarte's *Slide:ology* for a practical guide to color selection.

[8] Intensity combines two other aspects of color: saturation and lightness. The description of intensity in the text is closer to describing saturation. More precisely, a fully desaturated color would appear transparent to the background color, and a color with no lightness would appear black.

BEST PRACTICES FOR USING COLOR AS AN ENCODING
Use hue to distinguish categories and intensity to divide within categories
Stick with one hue for each category and vary the intensity to differentiate subcategories. The three examples in the figure show different ways of using hue to encode survey results, progressing from least intuitive to most intuitive.

Different hue for every segment
- Categories are easy to distinguish.
- Relationship between categories is not intuitive.

Single hue of increasing intensity
- Category progression is easier to see.
- Unintuitive that "Very dissatisfied" is less intense than "Somewhat dissatisfied."

Three hues with varying intensity
- Hue separates responses into dissatisfied in reds, neutral in gray, and satisfieds in blues.
- Intensity differentiates more extreme responses from less extreme responses.

How satisfied were you with your checkout process?

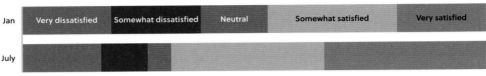

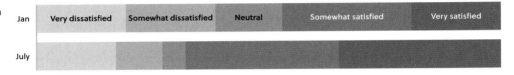

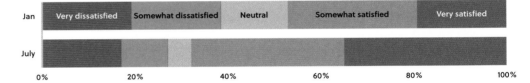

Use intensity to highlight elements within a category

Use intensity to focus the audience on a specific graphical element by making it more visually salient. In the graph, Region 4 stands out from the other regions on the right because it's a higher intensity shade of burgundy. If the focus of the discussion ought to be on Region 4, use intensity to direct the audience there.

INTENSITY HELPS ELEMENTS STAND OUT FROM OTHERS IN THEIR CATEGORY

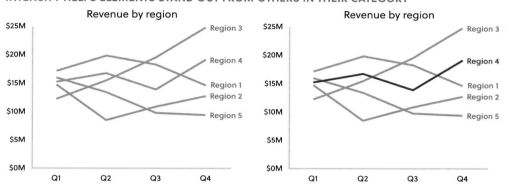

(Left) No region stands out. Region 3 is most salient because its label is in the highest position.

(Right) Region 4 stands out because its line and label are more intense.

Use a limited palette

Limit the number of hues to reduce cognitive load on the audience. The Curse of Knowledge is especially strong with hue. With practice, individuals can learn to map many different colors to different categories, but they struggle to interpret them quickly when the colors and categories are unfamiliar. This makes a large color palette useful for exploratory data visualization but dangerous when moving to explanatory visualization.

Use a colorblind-safe palette

If your audience consists of more than twenty people, it's likely that at least one of them has a color vision deficiency. Select hues that most viewers can distinguish, and check how the colors render on black-and-white printouts. Be careful of red/green and blue/green combinations, as these are the most common forms of color vision deficiency.

Consider using intensity to encode quantitative variables (and avoid rainbow palettes)

Use intensity to encode quantitative variables, rather than hue, and avoid rainbow palettes. Despite their widespread use in the scientific community, and their common use on weather maps, rainbow palettes are difficult to learn and should be avoided for explanatory visualizations.[9]

When using intensity to encode a quantitative variable, choose whether to map every value to a different level of intensity on a continuous scale or to group values into bins with a single shade covering a range of values. In general, opt for a continuous scale to better reflect the underlying data unless the context suggests discrete groupings, such as grades (where an A might be 90–100 and a B might be 80–89.9).

INTENSITY ENCODING OF VALUES

Continuous
For relative comparison

Bins
When values can be divided into discrete categories

Graphs create meaning using Gestalt principles

Understanding the preattentive attributes helps us understand how graphs encode variables visually. The Gestalt principles help us understand how audiences decode those visuals. In particular, they help us predict how audiences will chunk visuals together.

Gestalt principles emerged from the work of twentieth-century German psychologists who sought to explain an aspect of what we might now call chunking.[10] They wanted to explain the principles our minds use to create visual connections. Why do we see a dashed line as a line rather than a series of individual marks? Designers use the principles that emerged from this work to make products more intuitive. You can use them to make graphical choices that audiences can decode more reliably with lower cognitive load.

---

[9] The rainbow palette is used widely in science, engineering, and medicine. Like almost all encodings, an individual can learn to decode a rainbow palette easily with enough experience. Most people have learned to decode weather maps. However, even the common convention of mapping higher-wavelength light to higher values doesn't seem to make it easier for most people to intuit that the wavelength of yellow is longer than blue and therefore encodes a higher value. For one of many critiques of the rainbow color map, see Steve Eddins, "Rainbow Color Map Critiques: An Overview and Annotated Bibliography," *Mathworks.com*, 2014, https://www.mathworks.com/company/newsletters/articles/rainbow-color-map-critiques-an-overview-and-annotated-bibliography.html.

[10] Gestalt psychology focused on the nature of human perception and is distinct from the Gestalt approach to psychotherapy.

Four core Gestalt principles inform most graphs.[11]

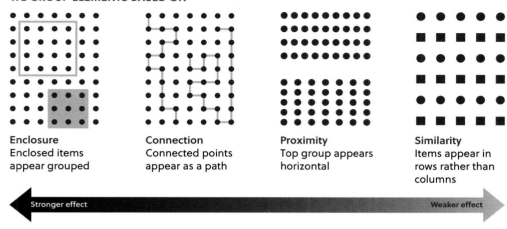

Enclosure
Enclosed items
appear grouped

Connection
Connected points
appear as a path

Proximity
Top group appears
horizontal

Similarity
Items appear in
rows rather than
columns

Stronger effect ← → Weaker effect

Some principles dominate others

Because some Gestalt principles dominate others visually, combining principles and vary-ing the intensity of different elements can change which elements are most salient and reorder how audiences tend to chunk them.

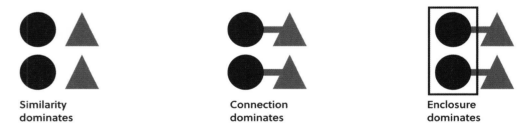

Similarity
dominates

Connection
dominates

Enclosure
dominates

Every pair in the example consists of a pair of circles and triangles. The circle and triangle are both similar in shape and hue. In the first pairing on the left, most people tend to see the shapes grouped into vertical pairs. They group the circles together as one chunk and the triangles together as a second chunk. In the middle pairing, the Gestalt principle of connection tends to dominate. Most people chunk this into two horizontally grouped pairs. The line connecting the circle and triangle overrides their similarity. In the final set on the right, the enclosure around the circles dominates the image, and most people focus entirely on the pair of circles.

---

[11] Other Gestalt principles include closure, symmetry, continuity, common fate, and past experience. Modern design-ers continue to add new principles, building on the foundation laid by the Gestalt theorists. This text focuses on a core set of laws that I think have the most application to static graphs. Like other visualization authors, I have also included a Law of Enclosure.

Let your understanding of Gestalt principles guide you to use them carefully. Because certain principles are so powerful, many are tempted to highlight key insights with bright circles and bold lines. Instead, opt for what Edward Tufte called the "smallest effective difference." Use the most subtle principle that achieves the desired effect, and you will create data visualizations that engage the audience without visually overwhelming them.

Enclosure

We perceive items that are visually enclosed as grouped together. Outlines and shaded regions are both examples of enclosures. Enclosures are powerful and should be avoided when emphasis can be added without the clutter enclosures generate.

BEST PRACTICES FOR USING ENCLOSURES

Use intensity and hue, not enclosures, to focus your audience on key points

Enclosures are one of the most visually overpowering ways to add emphasis. They tend to drown out other elements, including the ones they are designed to highlight. They are often added to graphs during the revision process by more senior managers looking to highlight a point quickly without having to redraw the graph. Instead of adding an enclosure to highlight a data point, consider deemphasizing all the other elements to make the key data more salient.

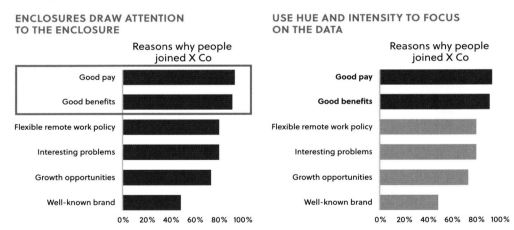

Use enclosure sparingly to group items

Enclosures are often used to group items. Even used sparingly, this effect can be overpowering. Avoid the temptation to add heavy boxes or circles for emphasis. This creates multiple salient points and obscures the power of any individual point. Try to create a hierarchy of information, from most important to least important, and use different levels of intensity to signal that hierarchy.

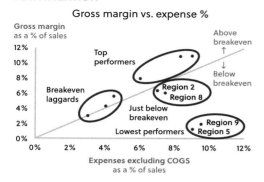

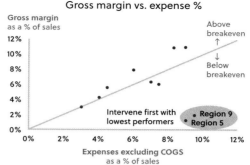

Connection

We perceive items that are visually connected as being grouped together. All line graphs take advantage of this principle by connecting individual points to create a sense of movement along a line, usually through time.

BEST PRACTICES FOR USING CONNECTION

Make sure visually connected points are conceptually connected

Time is most often encoded as a line because it mirrors the underlying concept of moving through time. Make sure that lines connect elements that are conceptually connected. The line on the left is an inappropriate way to depict this graph, because products are not conceptually connected to each other. Each product is a different category and would be better encoded with bars.

NO LOGICAL REASON TO CONNECT REGIONS

BARS ARE A MORE APPROPRIATE CHOICE

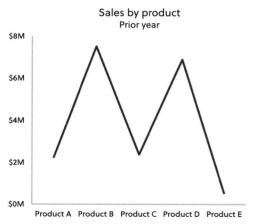

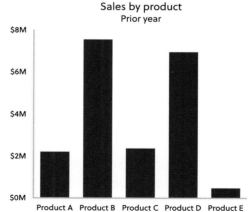

Proximity

We perceive items close together as members of a group.

BEST PRACTICES FOR USING PROXIMITY

Take advantage of proximity to avoid legends

Legends increase cognitive load on audience members, forcing their eyes to jump around to categorize graphical elements. Use proximity to lower cognitive load by labeling elements directly.

Put labels very close to the elements they identify

LEGENDS FORCE THE AUDIENCE TO SEARCH FOR KEY INFO

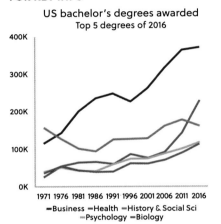

LABEL LINES DIRECTLY TO LOWER COGNITIVE LOAD

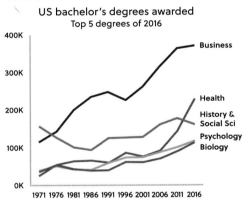

Source: U.S. Department of Education, National Center for Education Statistics, Higher Education General Information Survey (HEGIS)

The human eye is very sensitive to proximity. When labeling points or lines on the graph, place the label as close as possible to the element it identifies. Small changes in proximity can have a disproportionate impact on the audience's understanding.

Similarity

We perceive similar things as being grouped together. Take advantage of this principle to clarify connections. Using similar colors for the labels and the lines helps reinforce which label is associated with each line.

BEST PRACTICES FOR USING SIMILARITY

Use similarity to reinforce which element a label refers to

Match the hue between the label and the element it refers to in order to further reinforce the connection.

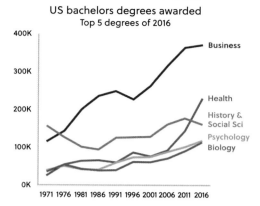

US bachelors degrees awarded
Top 5 degrees of 2016

Key concepts from this chapter

Humans are very good at seeing visual relationships, but we can only see one chunk of information at a time, and we are drawn to the most salient things.

WHAT WE SEE WHEN WE SEE GRAPHS

What we see	What it means	What it implies
Relationships	We see relationships, patterns, and exceptions to patterns.	Don't use a graph unless you are investigating or demonstrating a relationship.
Chunks	We mentally group visual elements into chunks and can only remember a few chunks of what we see.	Separate visual elements into a small number of distinct groups to help the audience decode them.
Salience	We see what is most prominent. Only one thing can be most prominent at a time.	Identify the most important element on the graph and make it the most visually prominent.

GRAPHS ENCODE DATA USING PREATTENTIVE ATTRIBUTES

Preattentive attribute	Tends to encode	Types of encodings	Best practices
Size	Values	Height, width, area	Start bars from zero and avoid y-axis truncation.
Position	Values	Points, lines, boxes	Encode up as good whenever possible.
Hue	Categories	Single hue, multiple hues	Use a limited, color-blind safe palette. Use hue to distinguish between categories.
Intensity	Categories, emphasis	Continuous, bins	Use intensity to divide within categories.

EFFECTIVE USE OF GESTALT PRINCIPLES HELPS MAKE GRAPHS EASIER TO DECODE

Gestalt principle	Examples	Best practices
Enclosure	Highlight boxes, shaded regions	Avoid enclosures for highlighting when intensity can be used.
Connection	Lines, pointers	Make sure visually connected points are conceptually connected.
Proximity	Labels, annotations	Label elements within the graph. Avoid legends and notes outside the graph when possible.
Similarity	Identifying categories by shapes or color	Match connected elements by using similar shape and hue.

If you remember nothing else . . .

The limitation on how many chunks we can actively hold in our brains is strict. We generally have space for three to four chunks at a time.

When we try to make everything salient, it turns everything into noise.

If the underlying data justifies more complexity, ask yourself if concepts can be split across multiple graphs to reduce cognitive load.

Exercise: Break down the graphs

Analyze the graphs below. Identify every preattentive attribute used to encode information and every Gestalt principle that helps clarify the organization of the graph. Look beyond the data plotted in the graph to see all the ways the designers try to help lower cognitive load on the reader. Remember that the same principle can be used multiple times in different ways.

GRAPH 1

U.S. markets

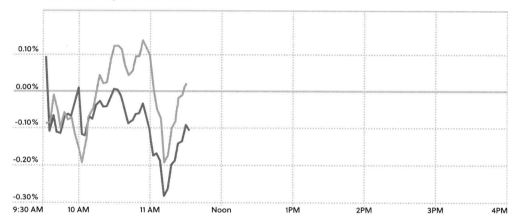

■ **S&P 500 Index**
2,864.16 -3.03 -0.11%

■ **Nasdaq**
7,830.81 +1.90 +0.02%

Source: Adapted from *The New York Times* Market Overview, https://markets.on.nytimes.com/research/markets/overview/overview.asp. Accessed 4/2/2019 at 11:34 am.

COMPLETE THE TABLES

Preattentive attribute	Encodes
Size (height, width & area)	
Position (points, lines, or boxes)	
Intensity	
Hue	

Gestalt principle	Clarifies
Enclosure	
Connection	
Proximity	
Similarity	

GRAPH 2

Student exercise habits

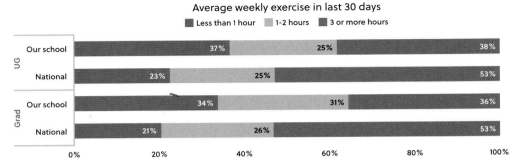

Average weekly exercise in last 30 days

■ Less than 1 hour   ■ 1-2 hours   ■ 3 or more hours

Exercising was defined as any exercise of moderate or higher intensity, where "moderate intensity" would be roughly equivalent to brisk walking or bicycling.

COMPLETE THE TABLES

Preattentive attribute	Encodes
Size (height, width & area)	
Position (points, lines, or boxes)	
Intensity	
Hue	

Gestalt principle	Clarifies
Enclosure	
Connection	
Proximity	
Similarity	

Part II

Designing Your Data

—

How to design effective graphs and slides

CHAPTER 3

Choose the Right Graph
(for your data)

——

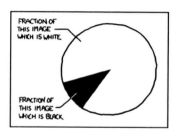 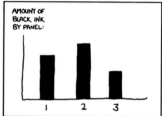 

Source: https://xkcd.com/688

Graphs rely on our ability to see relationships. So, selecting the best graph starts with understanding the data relationship you want to highlight. This chapter introduces the major types of relationships and then provides a deeper dive into the best practices for graphing each of them, including the common graph types used to show that relationship. At the end of the chapter, test your ability to recognize data relationships by categorizing and sketching graphs based on the relationship they ought to show.

Pick the graph based on the relationship

Graphs visualize relationships by chunking data and making the key comparisons visually salient. Identifying the underlying relationship is the key to choosing the appropriate type of graph. Strengthen your graph selection skills by first identifying the underlying relationship you want to highlight, and allow that relationship to guide your graph choice.

This chapter focuses on the most common relationships and graph types. These graphs cover most situations and are familiar to a wide variety of audiences. Their familiarity is a feature, not a bug. It allows audiences to decode them with less cognitive load, and most visualization tools support them. Use them to focus the audience on the underlying data, not the image you have used to encode it.[1]

---

[1] This book assumes the common workplace situation where your audience is invested in the decision your data addresses and where the primary goal of your communication is to transmit the underlying data as efficiently as possible. When you have a different goal for the visual, such as creating virality online, there are solid arguments for using uncommon graph forms and unusual designs. But for most day-to-day visualizations, you should reduce cognitive load with the clarity that comes from familiarity.

Relationship	Primary focus	Common examples	
Categorical	How the values of different categories compare at one moment in time	Bar graph	Clustered bar graph
Over time	How one or more categories of data change over time	Line graph	Bar graph
Part-to-whole	How different categories (or parts) form a whole	Stacked bar	Mosaic
Distribution	How observations within a category are distributed based on their measured value	Histogram	Box plot
Correlation	How the values of one variable relate to the values of a different variable for the same instance of the data	Scatterplot	Bubble graph

---

[2] This list and all the lists of common comparison words that follow are derived from Stephen Few's *Show Me the Numbers*, which was in turn based on Gene Zelanzy's *Say It with Charts*. Both are excellent reads. Few and others often include "sorting and ranking," "deviation from a baseline," and "geospatial" as common data relationships. Geospatial has been omitted here to reduce complexity and because not all graphing programs support mapping. "Sorting and ranking" is addressed within "categorical" and "part to whole" relationships because most people tend to mentally categorize sorting and ranking as special cases of these relationships. Similarly, "deviation" almost always includes a categorical or time component, so it is discussed within those sections.

Words that
signal categorial
relationships
Any quantitative
measure paired with
a category

Categorical relationships

Categorical relationships compare the value of one measure across different categories. These comparisons are the most common and most straightforward relationships you will encounter.

Example scenarios
- Revenue by product
- Graduation rates by undergraduate major
- Average deal size by salesperson
- Durability by fabric type
- Advertisement views by demographic group

Common graphs of categorical relationships
BAR GRAPHS
This common comparison is best visualized by the most common graph: the bar graph. Opt for the bar graph often to take advantage of your audience's familiarity with this graph type and the low cognitive load required to process it.

USE VERTICAL BARS BY DEFAULT

USE HORIZONAL BARS FOR LONG LABELS OR MANY ITEMS

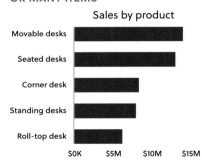

Use vertical bars when
- Making most categorical comparisons
- There are a limited number of items to compare
- Bar labels fit horizontally

Use horizontal bars when
- There are too many categories to fit vertically
- Category names would have to be slanted in order to fit a vertical graph
- Variety will reduce confusion among similar vertical bar graphs

CLUSTERED BARS

Clustered bars allow comparisons across two categories. Make sure that that the comparison is relevant before choosing this graph type. Use clusters only when they show a relationship that cannot be seen across two graphs.

To determine the clusters, decide which comparison is primary and which is secondary. The bars touching each other should be the primary comparison. This comparison is easier for the audience to see because it takes advantage of the Gestalt principle of connection.[3]

GROUPING BY YEAR FIRST FOCUSES ON HOW REGIONS COMPARE WITHIN A YEAR

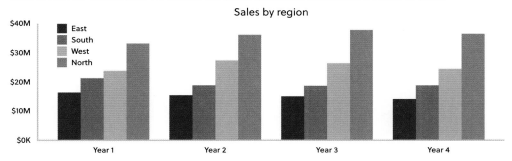

GROUPING BY REGION FIRST FOCUSES ON HOW EACH REGION HAS PERFORMED OVER TIME

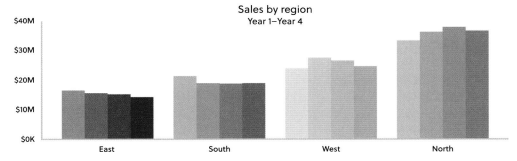

The examples compare the impact of different clustering choices. The primary comparison in the first graph is among the regions within each individual year. The comparison across the years is secondary.

In the second graph, the primary comparison is the performance within each individual region over the four years shown. The comparison among the regions is secondary, but it is easier to see on the second graph because the sales within each grouping vary less that they do in the first graph. Both comparisons are valid ways of organizing the data. Choose the grouping based on the comparison you want to emphasize.

---

[3] Gestalt principles are addressed in chapter 2.

BEST PRACTICES FOR SHOWING CATEGORICAL RELATIONSHIPS

Sort meaningfully (usually based on the data)

Always choose a meaningful sort order for the data. The data on the left is sorted alphabetically by category. The data on the right is sorted by values. Sorting by values allows the audience to evaluate the ranking of segments and makes comparisons easier. In general, sort categorical data by values unless another sorting will be meaningful for the audience.

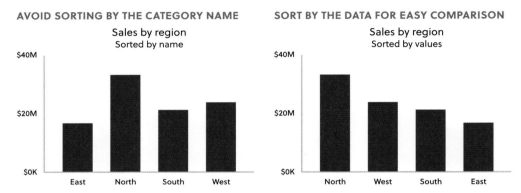

AVOID SORTING BY THE CATEGORY NAME

Sales by region
Sorted by name

SORT BY THE DATA FOR EASY COMPARISON

Sales by region
Sorted by values

Words that signal relationships over time
- Change
- Rise
- Increase
- Fluctuate
- Grow
- Decline
- Decrease
- Reduce
- Trend

Relationships over time

Relationships over time compare categories to themselves at different points in time. By convention, time is on the x-axis and flows from left to right.[4]

Example scenarios
- Product revenue growth
- Change in subscriber activity
- Throughput by time of day
- Trends in order volume
- Server uptime rates, trailing 30 days

---

[4] My sister-in-law, an accountant, was once asked to add some graphs to the annual report to "make it more interesting." After several rounds of edits from increasingly senior executives at her firm, the entire accounting team met with the CEO for the final sign off. The company's CEO politely requested that "the graphs please show time moving forward, as we hope our company will." The accountants had graphed time flowing from right to left. They quickly realized why none of them had noticed they had graphed time flowing in the "wrong" direction: accounting statements always show the most recent year or quarter on the left, closest to the text label. The accountants had built the graphs off of spreadsheets configured for accounting statements. The Curse of Knowledge blinded them to anything amiss.

Common graphs of relationships over time
LINE AND BAR GRAPHS

Relationships over time are usually shown as lines or bars. Each graph type emphasizes a different aspect of the data, because each divides the data into different chunks.[5] Lines emphasize the overall shape and trend of the data. Bars emphasize comparisons between individual values.

Because we tend to treat each line as a single chunk, the line graph below emphasizes the trend. This line graph supports conversations focused on the overall sales pattern across the year. The line emphasizes how monthly sales tend to increase as the year goes on. You could use this to facilitate a conversation about the increased staffing required in the later months of the year.

The bar graph of the same data emphasizes the individual months and deemphasizes the overall trend. Use bars to support conversations that focus on performance in specific months and how those months compare to each other. In the example, sales tend to increase in the last month of each quarter, which is common in organizations that compensate sales teams based on quarterly revenue goals. The bar graph could be used to argue for different sales incentives in the earlier months of each quarter to smooth out the trend.

CONTINUOUS LINES EMPHASIZE THE PATTERN OVER THE ENTIRE YEAR

DISCRETE BARS EMPHASIZE PERFORMANCE IN INDIVIDUAL MONTHS

Use continuous lines when
- The emphasis is on the overall shape of the data
- The conversation should focus on patterns and trends

Use discrete bars when
- The emphasis is on individual values
- The conversation should focus on the comparison between specific moments in time

---

[5] Chunking is addressed more thoroughly in chapter 2.

Best practices for showing relationships over time
KEEP TIME PERIODS EQUAL ALONG THE X-AXIS

Avoid varying the time period shown on the x-axis, and keep time periods even. If data collection was intermittent, visualize this with gaps in a line graph or an unconnected point for each observation. For comparing bars over different periods, create separate graphs that share a y-axis scale.

USE SEPARATE GRAPHS WITH THE SAME Y-AXIS SCALE WHEN COMPARING DIFFERENT TIME PERIODS

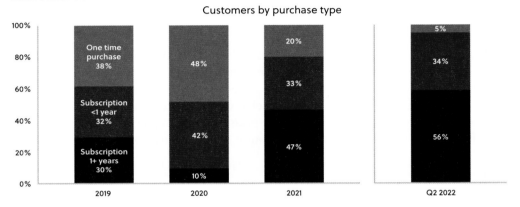

Customers by purchase type

CHOOSE A MEANINGFUL DISPLAY RATE

Displaying the data at the same rate it was collected—or presented to you—may not be the most effective way to show the underlying relationship to the audience. Data shown with intervals that are too frequent risk foregrounding noise that obscures the underlying pattern. Data shown with intervals that are too long between each period may omit patterns that the audience needs to understand. Let the nature of the relationship determine the most appropriate display rate.

The examples below compare the same data with different display rates. The graph on the left displays monthly data, which obscures a meaningful change in customer satisfaction for one product feature. The graph on the right compares just two periods. Here it emphasizes the overall trend and minimizes noise. This two-point line graph is called a slope graph.

**SHOWING TOO MANY INTERVALS
CAN OBSCURE TRENDS WHEN THERE
IS HIGH VARIABILITY**

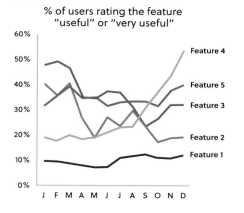

% of users rating the feature
"useful" or "very useful"

**REDUCE THE NUMBER OF INTERVALS
SHOWN TO EMPHASIZE THE OVERALL TREND**

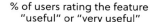

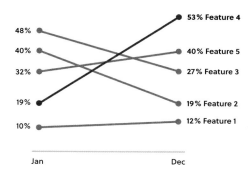

% of users rating the feature
"useful" or "very useful"

(Left) High variability
obscures the
audience's ability
to see trends.

(Right) Reduced
number of
measurement points
can clarify trends.

In the following graphs, the opposite is true. An infrequent display rate obscures a substantial variation in website traffic between weekends and the middle of the week.

**SHOWING TOO FEW INTERVALS CAN
OBSCURE IMPORTANT TRENDS**

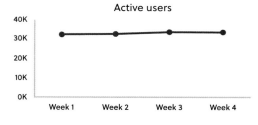

**SHOW MORE FREQUENT INTERVALS TO
REVEAL IMPORTANT PATTERNS**

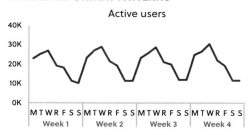

Words that signal
part-to-whole
relationships
• Share or share
  of total
• Percent or
  percentage of total
• Mix

Part-to-whole relationships

Part-to-whole relationships show both the breakdown of a whole into its component parts and the relative weights of those components. One of the first relationships you learned to graph was probably a part-to-whole relationship in the form of a pie chart.

Example scenarios
- Supplier share
- Cost breakdown
- Market landscape
- Customer mix

Common graphs of part-to-whole relationships

STACKED BARS

Part-to-whole relationship graphs take advantage of the Gestalt principle of connection to show that separate components taken together make up a whole. However, there is a trade-off between easy comparison of individual values and emphasizing how these parts form the entirety of the whole.

STACKED BARS EMPHASIZE HOW THE PARTS FORM THE WHOLE

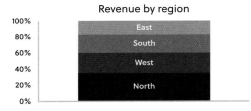

CLUSTERED BARS ALLOW FOR EASIER READING OF INDIVIDUAL VALUES

Note: Regions comprise 100% of company sales

Use stacked bars when
- The emphasis is on showing all the components that form the whole
- Sorting can be used to help the audience know which segments are bigger
- All components are included. Do not omit any components of the whole from this graph type

Use clustered bars when
- The emphasis is on the individual weight of each segment
- Not every component will be shown
- Additional labeling or context emphasizes that these segments add up to 100%

Compare the two examples above. The stacked bar on the left emphasizes that these four regions, taken together, represent 100% of the company's revenue. However, it's difficult to decode what percentage of sales each individual region contributes, other than the northern region, which can be read off the y-axis.

The graph on the right allows the audience to more easily read the value of individual bars, but it's less clear that these regions, taken together, form the entirety of the company's sales. It takes extra cognitive load to add the values together and check whether they add up to 100%. Be mindful of this kind of trade-off. Choose the graph type that emphasizes the more important aspect of the relationship and add annotation to point out other relevant details.

If the part-to-whole relationship is important enough to warrant additional cognitive load from the audience, two options for increased complexity are waterfall charts or mosaic charts (sometimes called mekkos).

WATERFALL CHARTS

Waterfall charts separate a stacked bar chart horizontally to emphasize how each category adds or subtracts from some base value. Unlike stacked bars, they allow for negative values and can illustrate the sequence in which the parts come together. Waterfalls can support additional encodings, like hue, without appearing as cluttered as a many-colored stacked bar.[6]

Use waterfalls when both inflows (like revenue) and outflows (like expense) comprise the whole. Waterfalls can also be valuable when there is some meaningful ordering to the components, such as in a step-by-step process.

WATERFALL CHARTS CAN SHOW BOTH POSITIVE AND NEGATIVE CONTRIBUTIONS TO THE WHOLE

Use waterfall charts when
- The whole includes positive and negative components
- An ordering other than by size adds meaning
- The audience is invested enough in the topic to tolerate substantial cognitive load

---

[6] Hue is explained in chapter 2. It maps most closely to the colloquial use of the word color, but it is differentiated here from other ways to adjust color, like intensity.

MOSAIC CHARTS (ALSO CALLED MEKKOS)

Mosaic charts are sometimes described as square pie charts. They use both height and width to encode data. The width of each vertical bar encodes the category value, and the height encodes the value of each segment within it. Like clustered bars, they support comparisons both within and across multiple categories. Mosaics encode a large amount of information in a small space. This data density makes them powerful for those trained to read them, but it introduces a substantial cognitive load on the uninitiated. Plan to spend a significant amount of time orienting audiences every time you present one.

MOSAIC CHARTS SHOW PART-TO-WHOLE COMPARISONS ACROSS TWO CATEGORIES ON ONE GRAPH

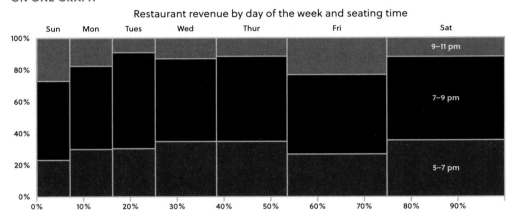

Use mosaic charts when
- Showing the part-to-whole relationship of two categories
- The audience will tolerate extensive explanation of this graph type

The example shows the revenue breakdown for a restaurant over the past week. Each day of the week is a column, and each column is subdivided by the three major seating times, 5–7 p.m., 7–9 p.m., and 9–11 p.m. The graph quickly shows that Friday and Saturday account for almost 50% of the week's revenue, and that 7–9 p.m. is the most popular dining window every day of the week.

These charts are sometimes called mekkos, a name derived from the Finnish textile and design company Marimekko, which is known for its bold multicolor geometric prints. They are often used to map markets with multiple segments and subsegments.

Best practices for showing part-to-whole relationships
MAKE SURE CATEGORIES TO BE COMPARED SHARE A COMMON BASELINE

One weakness of stacked bar charts is that the middle segments within the bars are hard to compare with each other, because they lack a common baseline. When creating stacked bar charts, remember that the audience can only easily compare bars that share a common baseline.

THE TOP SEGMENTS AND THE BOTTOM
SEGMENTS ARE EASIER TO COMPARE

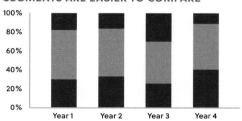

THE MIDDLE SEGMENTS ARE MORE
CHALLENGING TO COMPARE

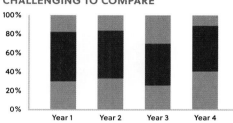

The top and bottom segments share a common baseline, making them easier to compare than the middle segments.

ORDER THE PARTS MEANINGFULLY

As with all categorical comparisons, you should order the segments in a part-to-whole comparison meaningfully—usually based on their value from largest to smallest. This helps audiences discriminate between similarly sized boxes.

Other orderings are reasonable as long as they are meaningful. The earlier mosaic graph of restaurant revenue is ordered by time—horizontally by days of the week and vertically from earliest seating to latest seating—rather than from largest to smallest segment. Even though this makes comparison of the 7–9 p.m. time slots challenging, time is a meaningful ordering for this data. It allows for a more intuitive comparison than ordering each day from largest revenue segment to smallest.

AVOID PIE CHARTS EXCEPT IN LIMITED CIRCUMSTANCES

The pie chart is one of the most widely recognized graph types. As one of the first charts most people learn, almost everyone can decode it as a visual representation of a part-to-whole relationship. Despite its benefits of familiarity, audiences face significant challenges decoding values efficiently from this type of graph.

The pie chart's weaknesses have led a substantial number of visualization experts to discourage—or even outright forbid—its use. It should be used sparingly after careful consideration of its drawbacks.

PIE CHARTS BECOME DIFFICULT TO READ WITH MORE THAN A FEW SEGMENTS

Banks by share of total assets ($USD)

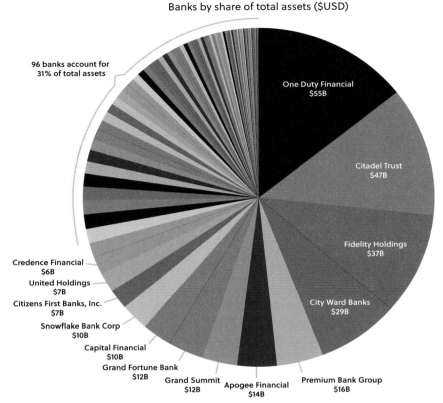

96 banks account for
31% of total assets

One Duty Financial
$55B

Citadel Trust
$47B

Fidelity Holdings
$37B

City Ward Banks
$29B

Credence Financial
$6B

United Holdings
$7B

Citizens First Banks, Inc.
$7B

Snowflake Bank Corp
$10B

Capital Financial
$10B

Grand Fortune Bank
$12B

Grand Summit
$12B

Apogee Financial
$14B

Premium Bank Group
$16B

Source: Names generated by FantasyNameGenerators.com

The two notable drawbacks to the pie chart are that it is difficult for audiences to compare precise segment sizes and that it is challenging to identify the segment labels for all but the largest segments. As shown in the example, segments of similar size are hard to compare in pie charts. The ordering of the wedges gives a hint at the relative size of each segment, but estimating the percentage value of any one segment is difficult. Also, pie charts quickly become difficult to label with more than a few segments, and the smallest segments are indecipherable.[7] In general, bar charts convey the same information with more precision and clarity.

The pie chart has one major advantage: familiarity. People know that it conveys a part-to-whole relationship and that these wedges taken together represent all the parts of the whole, even if the specific values of the segments are hard to decode.

[7] If you want to dive into the pie chart debate, there's no better place to start than with Robert Kosara. The results of his research with Drew Skau presented in "An Illustrated Tour of the Pie Chart Study Results" are illuminating, and the article itself models some great explanatory visualization.

Only consider the pie chart for limited situations. If all of the following are true, then it may be worth it to use the pie chart

- There are a small number of segments in the pie
- The difference between the segments is large and easy to see
- There are no small segments (or they can be combined into an "Other" category)
- The overwhelming focus is on showing all the parts of the whole, rather than a comparison between segments
- The audience is unused to seeing information graphically

Distributions

Distributions show how a single category breaks down by the quantitative value of the items within that category. They are often confused with part-to-whole relationships. Distributions must subdivide a single category into ranges based on the value that category measures, like size of organization or purchase price. Part-to-whole comparisons divide the data by categories, like regions or vendors, rather than quantitative measures within a category like order size or response time. Graphing distributions is most useful when the items in a category are not normally distributed.[8]

Words that signal distribution relationships
- Frequency
- Concentration
- Distribution
- Range
- Normal curve, normal distribution, or bell curve

Example scenarios
- Purchase-size distribution
- Response-time breakdown
- Kilowatt consumption range

Common graphs of distribution relationships
HISTOGRAMS AND FREQUENCY POLYGONS
The most common way to graph a distribution is as a histogram. Histograms separate the data into different value ranges, called bins. By convention, histograms are drawn with no gaps between the bars. Audiences may not recognize that this convention signals a histogram, unless they use statistical analysis software. Be prepared to carefully label and explain this graph type.

An alternate way to compare multiple distributions is by graphing each distribution as a line, as shown in the right-hand graph that follows. Line graphs that show distributions, rather than changes over time, are called frequency polygons. Like all line graphs, frequency polygons get confusing when there are too many categories or when the categories cross over each other often—so limit the number of categories.

---

[8] The "bell curve" is a visual representation of a normal distribution.

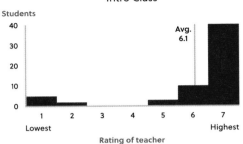

Student ratings for Prof. Kelly,
Intro Class

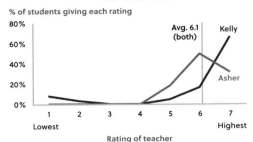

Student ratings distribution
for Intro Class

Use histograms when
- Showing the distribution of a single variable
- The audience is familiar with histograms

Use lines when
- Comparing the distribution of multiple variables
- Variables are of comparable scale or can be converted to percentages
- Labeling and context reduce the chance it will be confused for a time series

BOX PLOTS

Introduced in the late 1960s, box plots are a more recent innovation in data visualization. They usually require extensive explanation with business audiences, because they come in many varieties and require some intuitive understanding of statistical abstractions, like quartiles.

The example box plot compares the salary ranges of one company's employees based on their roles. Each category is divided into two boxes. The line between the boxes is the median salary for that position. The bottom box goes from the lowest salary for employees in that position to the median salary. The top box shows the range from median to highest salary. This box plot allows the audience to see that the median salary for sales managers is slightly lower than the median salary for marketing managers, but the range of salaries for sales managers is much wider. The highest-paid sales manager makes substantially more than the highest-paid marketing manager.

Use box plots when the audience has an academic research background—where they are much more common. They are most useful when the data demands a comparison of multiple distributions, a frequency polygon would be too confusing, or a summary measure like an average is insufficient to describe the data.

One caveat to box plots is that the underlying data must be statistically monomodal. Monomodal distributions, when plotted on a histogram, have only one peak. One value or range is clearly dominant. If the average grade on a test is an 80 because most students scored in the 75–85 range, the distribution is monomodal. If half the students scored over 90 and the other half scored below 70, the distribution is bimodal—it has two peaks. A single average doesn't describe the class's performance very well. Box plots cannot effectively represent bimodal distributions because boxes can't represent two peaks.

BOX PLOTS CONDENSE MANY STATISTICAL MEASURES INTO A SINGLE IMAGE

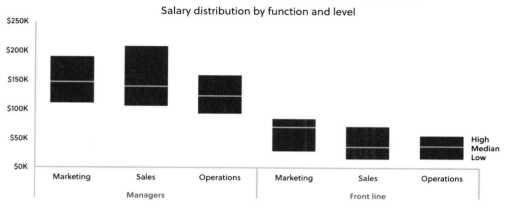

Use box plots when

- Comparing distributions across many categories
- The data is monomodal
- Only a few bins are needed to describe each distribution (in the graph above, each category is divided into two bins: one bin is for the range of salaries lower than the median and the other bin is for the range of salaries greater than the median)
- The relative size of the categories is not significant to the point of the graph (the front-line staff in this hypothetical organization is 50x larger than the managerial staff)
- There is time to orient audiences unfamiliar with this graph type
- The audience is familiar with statistical abstractions like quartiles

Best practices for showing distribution relationships
CHOOSE BINS THOUGHTFULLY

In histograms, dividing the data into equally sized bins creates the most intuitive separation for the audience, but this sometimes obscures critical patterns. Use irregularly sized bins when the underlying data justifies the division. The two histograms below show an alternate view of the salary data from the box plot above. The one on the left sizes the bins into evenly sized $50,000 ranges. The one on the right sizes the bins based on the pay bands set by HR. Though the graph on the right has uneven bin sizes, it provides a more accurate picture of employee pay ranges by focusing on the ranges where most employees' salaries fall. The sizing can be justified to the audience, since it is not arbitrary.

(Left) Evenly sized bins hide a relevant distinction between employees making less than $30K per year and those making $30–50K.

(Right) Bins based on HR pay ranges provide more detail in the salary ranges for most employees.

CHOOSE BINS THAT REFLECT MEANINGFUL DIVISIONS IN THE UNDERLYING DATA

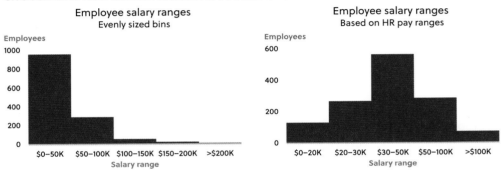

Words that signal correlation relationships
- Increases with
- Decreases with
- Changes with
- Varies with
- Correlated with
- Follows

Correlations

Correlations show the relationship between two quantitative variables. They are most often graphed as scatterplots.

Example scenarios
- Average order size impact on average order frequency
- Profitability and growth rate by region
- Salesperson tenure and amount sold
- Call length vs. quality rating
- Shovel sales by predicted snowfall

Words that signal causation and should be used with care

A better understanding of cause and effect is a common goal for business analysis. Hopefully, this improved understanding leads people to make choices that cause the desired effects. Correlations are a critical tool in that understanding, because they show how changes in one measure correlate with another measure. However, as every statistics professor warns, correlation does not equal the causation most managers seek to understand.

Be very careful when jumping from words that signal that two variables are correlated with each other to language making the more audacious claim that changes in one measure cause the changes in another measure.[9] Watch out for expressions like:

- Caused by
- Effected by
- Driven by
- Impact on

Common graphs of correlation relationships
SCATTERPLOTS

Scatterplots are the most common way to graph correlations. They show the relationship between two quantitative variables. Scatterplots have the advantage of allowing the audience to see individual data points, rather than statistical summaries like averages. When labeled and annotated well, they can be a powerful tool for explaining the data.

SCATTERPLOTS SHOW THE RELATIONSHIP BETWEEN TWO QUANTITATIVE VARIABLES

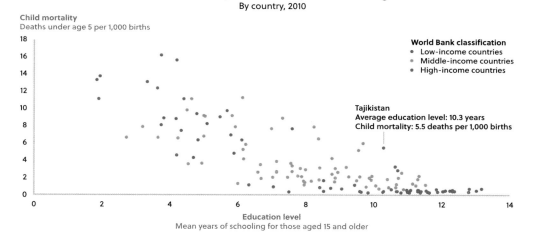

Child mortality rate vs. mean years of schooling
By country, 2010

Source: "Global Rise of Education" Max Roser and Esteban Ortiz-Ospina. Published online at OurWorldInData.org (2019)

---

[9] To paraphrase yet another memorable idea from Edward Tufte: while the world is three-dimensional and multivariate, graphs simplify that complexity to two-dimensional, univariate representations. In the process of simplification, nuance is always lost.

Use scatterplots when
- There is value in showing every data point
- Averages or statistical summaries might obscure key information
- There is a meaningful relationship between the two variables
- Outliers are either meaningful or minimal
- There is time to properly label and annotate the plot

BUBBLE CHARTS

While scatterplots show how two quantitative variables correlate, bubble charts use variation in the size of the points to encode a third quantitative variable. Our ability to compare area is less precise than our ability to compare height, so bubble sizes provide, at best, a rough measure of small versus large. When using this encoding, don't expect audiences to be able to estimate the bubble value.

Bubble charts can show far fewer points than scatter plots, but they are useful when the graph is designed to highlight clusters of points rather than correlation between the variables. In general, opt for scatterplots unless the information encoded in bubble size is critical for the decision the graph is designed to support.

The following graph is a market growth versus market share matrix. Consultants at the Boston Consulting Group developed this comparison to help conglomerates visualize how divisions of a conglomerate can function as a portfolio of investments. Rather than emphasizing a correlation between market share and market growth, its purpose is to help the audience mentally categorize the divisions in order to better allocate resources among them.

When using scatterplots or bubble charts to categorize or show clusters, explicitly label the regions or clusters to help the audience more effectively decode groupings. In the graph below each category has both a name, like "Cash Cow," and a description, like "low share; high growth," that helps explain the region. Help the audience decode the graph by providing explanations for the data close to the data itself.

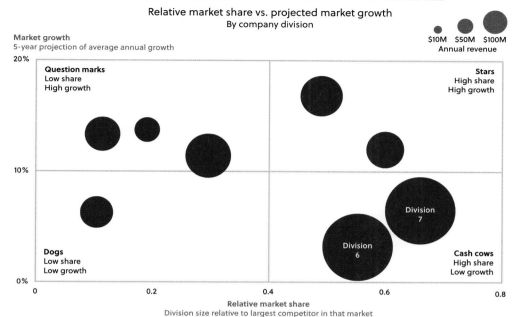

BUBBLE CHARTS ALLOW YOU TO ENCODE A THIRD VARIABLE VIA THE BUBBLE SIZE

Relative market share vs. projected market growth
By company division

$10M $50M $100M
Annual revenue

Market growth
5-year projection of average annual growth

Question marks
Low share
High growth

Stars
High share
High growth

Division 7

Division 6

Dogs
Low share
Low growth

Cash cows
High share
Low growth

Relative market share
Division size relative to largest competitor in that market

The relative market share of the market leader is 1.0. A competitor with 60% of the revenue of the market leader has a relative market share of 0.6.

Use bubble charts when
- There are a limited number of points
- Differences between the bubble sizes are significant and easy to distinguish
- The information encoded in bubble size is critical for the decision this graph supports
- There is time to properly label and annotate the plot
- The audience is familiar with this graph type or there is time to explain it

TABLE LENS
One alternative to the scatterplot is the table lens.[10] A table lens uses matched bar charts to show correlations. Though initially developed for interactive visualizations, the table lens is useful because it presents correlations as two bar charts—a graph type with which all audience members will probably be familiar. It is also useful in environments where a scatterplot may be difficult to read, such as large auditoriums.

---

[10] This display is recent enough to warrant a citation to its creators. Though initially designed for interactive visualizations, new visualization tools make it easier to create these for static visualizations. Still, creating one in Excel is tricky. It's worth searching for step-by-step instructions online if you don't create them frequently. Ramana Rao and Stuart K. Card, "The Table Lens," *Conference on Human Factors in Computing Systems Proceedings* (Apr. 1994): 318.

The main weakness of the table lens is that it can only show correlation in a very general way. The shape of the relationship between the points is lost. It cannot show clusters and groupings effectively, and it becomes unreadable with far fewer data points than a scatterplot can support.

TABLE LENSES SHOW CORRELATIONS OF A SMALL NUMBER OF POINTS IN A MORE COMMON GRAPHICAL FORMAT

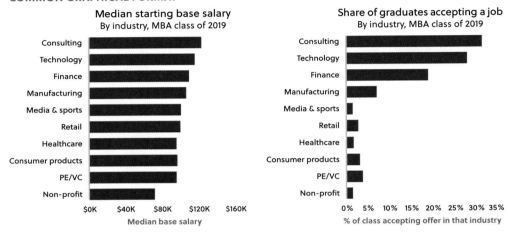

Note: Only includes base salary. Variable compensation and bonus may increase total pay substantially in many industries, especially in Finance and PE/VC.
Source: MBA Employment Office

Use table lenses when
- You have a small number of data points
- Using summary statistics, like averages, will not obscure key trends in the data
- Audiences are unfamiliar with scatterplots
- The correlation between the variables is clear

Best practices for showing correlation relationships
ADD BEST-FIT LINES AND ADDRESS OUTLIERS TO FOCUS THE AUDIENCE
One strength of scatterplots lies in their ability to support higher-density data. They pack a large amount of information into a small space. This can add substantial cognitive load for viewers if they are not sure where to look, so focus your audience on the key relationship with best fit lines. Address outliers so that the audience can process these inevitable distractions and return to the key point.

Best-fit lines allow the audience to visualize the conceptual point you want to make. They make it possible for the audience to literally "see" the conclusion you believe the data supports. As such, they are a very powerful tool and should be used only when you have strong evidence that the change on the x-axis variable causes the change in the y-axis variable.[11]

In addition to using best-fit lines to focus the audience, label and address outliers to minimize their distraction. Just as humans tend to see patterns, we are equally quick at spotting outliers. By definition, outliers are salient because they stand out. Since we focus on what is salient, make sure to label and explain any obvious outliers in your data. You may also choose to reduce the salience of outliers by reducing their intensity, as shown below. Avoid the temptation to leave them unaddressed. Confront them head-on so that you can satisfy your audience's need for explanation and direct their focus back to the key information.

VISUALIZE THE KEY RELATIONSHIPS AND ADDRESS OUTLIERS

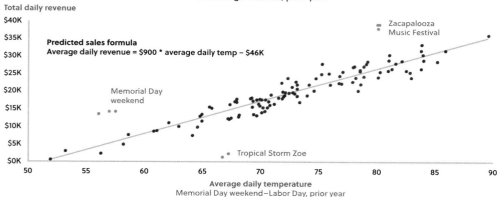

Ezra's Ice Cream Shoppe daily revenue by average temperature
Cambridge location, prior year

Predicted sales formula
Average daily revenue = $900 * average daily temp − $46K

Label outliers and reduce their intensity. This allows the audience to understand them and then return to the main idea of the graph.

Note: Sales prediction based on ordinary least squares linear regression.
Sales formula components are rounded to the nearest $1K for clarity. $R^2 = 0.83$
Source: Company Financial Reports; NOAA Climate Data Online

- Displaying the best-fit line draws attention to the correlation between temperature and ice cream sales.
- Formatting the equation of the best-fit line helps explain its meaning to a business audience.
- Labeling outliers helps explain them and refocuses the audience on the underlying pattern.
- Reducing the visual intensity of outliers decreases their salience.

---

[11] For a reminder on the danger of assuming causation based on correlation, scroll through Tyler Vigen's hysterical (by data-visualization standards) website: https://www.tylervigen.com/spurious-correlations.

FOCUS ON CORRELATION, NOT LACK OF CORRELATION

In general, focus explanatory presentations on what is correlated, not what isn't. Avoid showing uncorrelated variables except when necessary. The human inclination to find patterns can lead audiences to see correlation even in statistically uncorrelated variables.[12] If you must demonstrate a lack of correlation, avoid best-fit lines and other signals of correlation. In the figure below, the point of the plot is that a salesperson's experience—measured in years they have worked at the company—does not predict the sales they generate. In other words, more experience does not lead to more sales. An R^2 value of 0.008 says that tenure explains only eight-tenths of a percent of the variation in sales performance, but the upward sloping trend line can lead audiences to infer that there is a meaningful (if small) correlation between tenure and sales performance, even though there is none in this organization. This graph's point would be better made without the best-fit line.

AUDIENCES TEND TO SEE PATTERNS EVEN WHEN THERE ARE NONE

The best fit line suggests a correlation that isn't there.

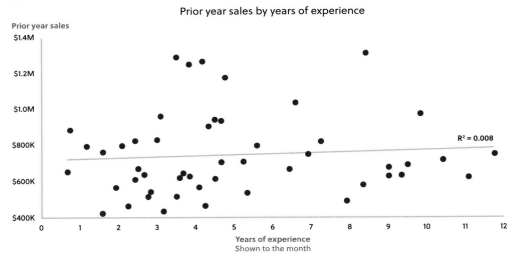

Prior year sales by years of experience

* In general, avoid showing lack of correlation unless it is required to understand the point of your communication.
* Don't show best-fit lines or other signifiers of correlation if the variables are not correlated.

---

[12] The tendency of humans to see patterns in unfamiliar information is well documented enough to have a name: apophenia. There are even names for specific subtypes of this inclination. Interpreting random images and sounds into recognizable patterns is called pareidolia. The most common example of pareidolia is our tendency to see faces, even in combinations of simple shapes like this: ☺.

Use taxonomies to expand your library of graph types

This chapter introduces the major relationships and most common graph types. The graph types here cover most graphs you will create to persuade others with data. In general, stick to common graph types whenever possible to ease the cognitive load on the audience. Allow the audience to focus on the data, not the visual itself.

When you are unsure how to show a specific relationship, need some inspiration because a common graph type feels insufficient, or aren't sure which software supports the chart type, multiple taxonomies exist online to help sharpen your skills and increase the breadth of graph types you can use. They are a powerful resource.

Taxonomy	Link	Organized by	Major benefits
Which Visualization?	Experception.net	The nature of the data (discrete vs. continuous)	• Quick and easy to use • Includes commentary on best practices
Financial Times Vocabulary	Ft.com/vocabulary	The type of relationship you want to highlight	• Updated regularly • Extensive • Maintained in English, Chinese & Japanese
The Graphic Continuum	Policyviz.com/product/the-graphic-continuum-desktop-sheet	The type of relationship you want to highlight	• Includes less common chart types for inspiration
The Chartmaker Directory	Chartmaker.visualisingdata.com	Visualization software package	• Compares functionality of all major visualization software

Key concepts from this chapter

Graphs show relationships. The key to picking the right graph is identifying the relationship the audience needs to understand.

COMMON RELATIONSHIPS VISUALIZED IN GRAPHS

Relationship	Visualizes	Common forms	Best practices
Categorical	How the values of different categories compare at one moment in time	Bars Clustered bars	• Default to vertical bars. • Use horizonal bars for long labels or many items. • Sort meaningfully.
Over time	How one or more categories of data change over time	Lines Bars	• Emphasize the overall pattern of change with lines. • Emphasize individual values with bars. • Maintain equal time periods. • Choose an appropriate display rate.
Part-to-whole	How different categories (or parts) form a whole	Stacked bars Waterfalls Mosaics	• Avoid pie charts except in limited circumstances. • Sort meaningfully. • Make sure categories to be compared share a common baseline.
Distribution	How observations within a category are distributed based on their measured value	Histograms Lines Box plots	• Use histograms to visualize a single distribution. • Use lines or boxes to visualize multiple distributions. • Choose meaningful bins.
Correlation	How the values of one variable relate to the values of a different variable for the same instance of the data	Scatterplots Bubble graphs Table lenses	• Address outliers explicitly. • Add best fit lines to demonstrate correlation. • Avoid showing plots to demonstrate lack of correlation.

If you remember nothing else . . .

Identify the relationship first, then choose the graph type.

Keep it simple. Only choose complex when the needs of the audience demand it.

People see outliers and patterns. Address outliers explicitly so the audience can move on, and avoid showing lack of correlation.

Exercise: Categorize the relationships

You are working with a teammate to plan out various slides in a presentation. You know what you want to show on each slide and what data you have available. Sketch out the graphical form that best displays the data.

Use the summary table at the beginning of the chapter to help guide you as you work through each potential slide below. Each graph has a goal and the data available to you. Based on the goal and the description of the data, identify the type of relationship the graph should highlight, and then sketch out a potential graph for that data. Make assumptions about how you think the data is likely to look and focus on the overall comparison rather than perfect design. Use this as a chance to think through alternative graph forms that could also support these conversations.

Goal of the graph and data available	Identify the relationship	Sketch the graph(s)
Goal: Demonstrate that the company's sales growth is highest in the Asia Pacific region of the world **Data: Sales by region over the last ten years**	Categorical (with a time component)	**Bar graph comparing growth rates** Pros: Simple. Emphasizes key relationship. Cons: Obscures relative magnitude of regions. **Line graph of sales for each region with growth rates labeled** Pros: Shows relative magnitude. Cons: May obscure growth rate if Asia Pacific is much smaller than other regions. May be confusing if lines cross. Labeling must be clear. **Clustered bar graph with the region as primary cluster** Pros: Shows relative magnitude of each component. May make it easier to compare regions if many lines would cross over each other. Cons: Harder to compare regions with each other than a line graph would likely be. Emphasizes values of specific years rather than the trend. **To avoid: clustered bars with year as the primary cluster** Clustering by year focuses on comparing the regions to each other within a specific year, rather than their growth over time.

Multiple graph types are appropriate for this scenario. The text here describes possible answers and evaluates their pros and cons. After sketching your graph, try to evaluate its pros and cons.

Goal of the graph and data available	Identify the relationship	Sketch the graph(s)
Goal: Show that the company's largest product category is 40% of overall sales with no single dominating product, and that the other categories each have one dominant product representing most of the sales **Data:** Sales by product and category for the prior five years		
Goal: Show that order size predicts the length of time before a customer's subsequent purchase (assume this is true) **Data:** Order sizes for all orders over the last fifteen years		

Goal of the graph and data available	Identify the relationship	Sketch the graph(s)
Goal: Show how call lengths differ among the four different call centers, despite the same average call time Data: Call lengths for every call to every call center for the last year		
Goal: Show that manufacturing error rates increase during school holiday weeks Data: Error volume and overall volume by day for the last year		

Goal of the graph and data available	Identify the relationship	Sketch the graph(s)
Goal: Demonstrate the relationship between customer satisfaction and lifetime value (the total amount a customer spends with the company) **Data:** Customer satisfaction scores and projected lifetime value of every customer for the last seven years		
Goal: Compare a valuation model's prediction of a company's value to its current market capitalization. Show the sources of difference visually **Data:** Output of a valuation model divided by sources of value and cost		

Goal of the graph and data available	Identify the relationship	Sketch the graph(s)
Goal: Compare revenue trends over the last year between two different divisions Data: Monthly revenue for each division over the last year		

Simplify to Amplify

(your message)

—

Source: https://xkcd.com/1983

Even thoughtfully built graphs fail to persuade the audience when they are burdened by needless clutter and excess complexity. The goal is not to reduce the complexity of the data your graph visualizes. The goal is to create graphs that are perfectly transparent windows into the underlying data. This chapter presents two approaches to simplifying your graphs and amplifying your message: maximizing the data–ink ratio and creating an information hierarchy. The exercise tests your ability to amplify the data by reducing clutter.

Maximize the data–ink ratio

Efficient graphs are clear graphs. They maximize the value of every mark on the page or pixel on the screen. Edward Tufte calls the graphical version of this relationship the "data–ink ratio." Your job is to maximize this ratio. Make sure every spot of ink on your graph conveys something about the underlying data. Doing so requires you to be ruthless about eliminating graphical elements that don't add clarity and disciplined about maximizing the value of all that remains.

Below are some common sources of excess ink and some critical steps to maximize the value of the ink that remains. Let the data and the nature of the comparison drive the very occasional exceptions to these rules. For example, use 3D graphs when it's appropriate to show three-dimensional data.

Minimize non-data ink	Maximize data ink
Eliminate all elements below except when essential to the meaning of the graph	Make sure to include all elements below unless they would be trivial to all audiences
✕ 3D and shadow effects	✓ Axis labels
✕ Borders and boxes	✓ Graph titles
✕ Large gaps between bars	✓ Readable font sizes
✕ Meaningless variations in color	✓ Data selection criteria
✕ Overpowering gridlines	—e.g., Top 6 Performing Regions
✕ Point markers on lines	✓ Sources
✕ Tick marks	✓ Unit labels on axis values
✕ Unnecessary significant digits	—e.g., $1M, $2M, $3M . . .

Remove non-data ink that creates clutter

The most common form of excess ink is clutter—visual elements that don't convey any meaning. Removing clutter has no impact on the elements that remain. Other excess visual elements may add some clarity—such as heavy gridlines—but the cognitive load they bring with them isn't worth the trade-off. Start mentally from a blank page, and make every element on your graph justify its existence to a hypothetical audience.

Note all the sources of clutter and excess ink in this deliberately awful graph.

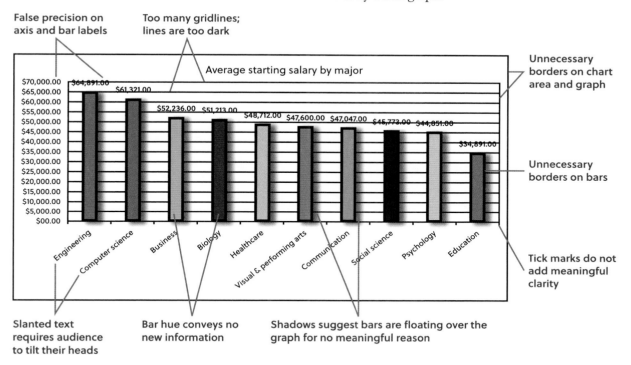

The next version of the graph removes the excess ink and clutter from the graph above. It is clearer than the first version,[1] but strengthening the power of the ink that remains could lower the cognitive load on the audience even further.

---

[1] Clutter doesn't just add confusion, it can reduce the accuracy of the data. The extra zeros on the salary values in the original graph are both technically inaccurate and misleading. They are inaccurate because the averages are rounded to whole numbers. The precise calculation of the average would extend out many decimal places. Showing precise values, to the cent, also makes them misleading. Averages are statistical summaries of ranges. Presenting them as precise values suggests all engineering graduates make exactly the same amount of money, rather than a range centered roughly around $65,000.

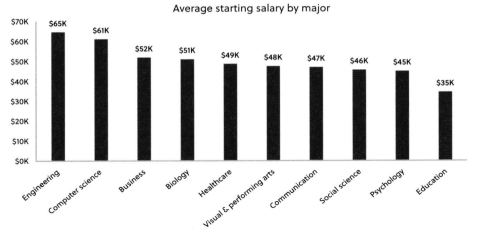

WITH LESS CLUTTER AND EXCESS, THE GRAPH SHOWS THE UNDERLYING DATA MORE CLEARLY

Average starting salary by major

WATCH OUT: One person's clutter is another person's credibility

Familiarity reduces cognitive load. It's easier for us to process information and graphical forms we've seen before. This is how the Curse of Knowledge works. We forget what it was like to be an audience exposed to something for the first time. While reducing excess ink can reduce cognitive load on audiences unfamiliar with the data, it can have the opposite effect on audiences who are used to seeing data in specific formats.

For example, research scientists who spend every workday using statistical analysis software packages may find it harder to decode a "cleaned-up" graph. The absence of lines they are used to seeing and the presence of labels in unfamiliar positions may add to their cognitive load. This increase in cognitive load may even cause them to question the credibility of the analyst and the analysis itself.[2]

Effective communication is about knowing your audience. Take the time to understand how an audience usually receives data. Don't let your knowledge of the best practices for communicating with audiences who are unfamiliar with the data get in the way of making the right choices for specific individuals. Or, to put it another way: regardless of what this book says, if your boss likes data shown in a certain way, format it that way for them.

---

[2] In one of my prior workplaces, engineers and scientists used to call decluttered graphs "marketing graphs." In case it's not clear from context, this was not a compliment. When creating graphs for this audience, we learned to leave in a few gridlines and some labeling that wasn't strictly necessary.

Maximize data ink that conveys information

After removing all the non-data ink, maximizing the impact of the data ink that remains requires thoughtful consideration of your audience's needs. The next section walks you through a checklist of graphical choices you can make to lower the audience's cognitive load and allow them to focus on the data the graph shows, not the graph itself.

Avoid slanted text

Slanted text is significantly harder to read than horizonal text.[3] The slanted labels in the prior salary graph add cognitive load. The graphs that follow demonstrate two common strategies to ease the burden on your audience: either shorten the data labels with common abbreviations, or use horizontal bars, which can accommodate more categories and longer text labels. Though there is some evidence that vertical bars are slightly easier to compare than horizontal ones, the benefits of horizontal text outweigh the minor drawbacks of horizontal bars.

USING COMMON ABBREVIATIONS CAN CREATE SPACE FOR HORIZONTAL LABELS

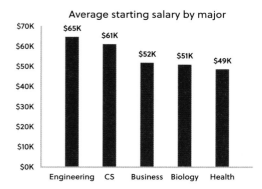

USING HORIZONTAL BARS CAN CREATE SPACE FOR LONGER LABELS AND MORE CATEGORIES

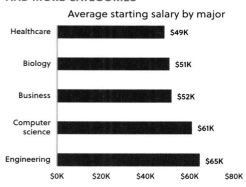

---

[3] Though it can be amusing to watch a room full of people simultaneously cock their heads 45 degrees to read your slide.

Label key elements with readable text

Clear labeling allows your readers to quickly identify what this visualization encodes. Create clarity both by labeling all the elements of the graph as well as by choosing font sizes that are readable in your audience's environment (on a laptop, on a printout, projected in a conference room). Increasing the legibility of the text is the single fastest way to decrease cognitive load. Err on the side of a font that is too large rather than a font that is too small.

The graph below adds credibility to the data via clarity. The data seems more trustworthy because the audience understands the topic of the graph, the source of the data, what the axes represent, and how the data was selected.[4]

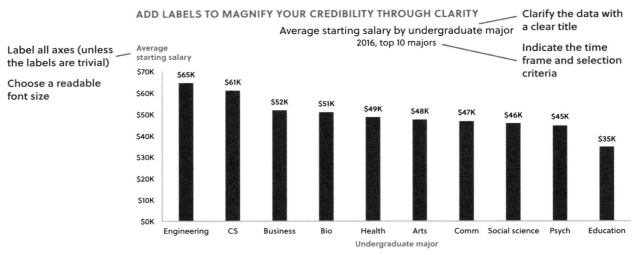

Reduce the gap width (to focus the audience on the data)

One subtle but profound way to increase the power of your data is to widen the bars. This focuses the audience on the data rather than the spaces between the data, and allows for easier comparison. There is no standard best practice, but in general aim to make the bars bigger than the gaps in between them.

---

[4] There is a strong argument for removing the y-axis label here. It's redundant given the title. On the other hand, axis labels are such familiar ink that their absence can trigger many audiences to question the credibility of the graph. If the label is truly obvious to the entire audience, omit it. For presentations where this data is shown on a large screen, make sure the axis label is in horizontal text above the axis for easier reading.

Here's a version of the graph with the gap width set to 67%. Note how the larger bar size focuses the audience on the bars, not the white space that separates them.

WIDER BARS ALLOW FOR EASIER COMPARISON

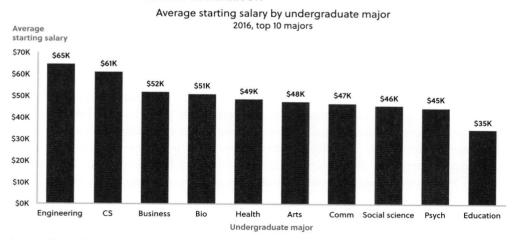

Average starting salary by undergraduate major
2016, top 10 majors

Source: Sallie Mae, from Statista.com

Make the most important information the most salient

The human brain avoids cognitive load, and the human visual processing system can see only a few things at a time. In particular, our visual system gravitates to whatever is most salient. As discussed in chapter 2, salience is the quality of "standing out."

Effective graphs—and slides, as discussed later—create an information hierarchy. They align the salience of the visual elements with their importance. Make the most important element the most visually salient and avoid the temptation to make multiple elements equally salient. If multiple things compete for our attention, nothing stands out. Instead, order visual elements from most prominent to least prominent. This reduces the number of visual elements your audience has to process at once, allowing graphs to support higher complexity.

TAKE A STRATEGIC APPROACH TO DESIGNING YOUR VISUAL HIERARCHY

Design element	Make elements more salient by
Size	Making the more important text larger
Type	Using **bold**, *italics*, underlining, CASE, and color in moderation to emphasize key words and concepts
Labels	Selectively labeling critical data points
Highlights	Increasing the color intensity of select data points
Reference lines	Including reference lines and regions to focus the key comparison
Annotation	Annotating key events or addressing outliers
Splitting	Separating graphs to avoid double y-axis graphs

To create this hierarchy, you must choose which aspects of the comparison are most important for the specific audience and context. The power of an effective explanatory visual emerges from these choices. Choices designed to increase the audience's clarity will increase your credibility with the audience. Choices intended to obscure data that weakens your conclusion will undermine your persuasive power even faster.

Since these clarifying choices serve the needs of a specific audience in a specific context, the highest-quality explanatory graphics aren't reusable. A change in audience, context, or topic changes the optimal visual choices.

Enlarge the more important text

Making something larger than the elements around it is one of the easiest ways to increase its salience. In this example, the focus of this graph for this audience is on the starting salaries of different majors. Increasing the font size of the graph title draws the audience's eyes to this crucial information, which is required to make sense of the rest of the graph. Decreasing the size of the source and axis labels increases the prominence of the majors, which are the main categories we want the audience to compare.

VARY THE TEXT SIZE TO START THE AUDIENCE WITH THE MOST IMPORTANT INFORMATION

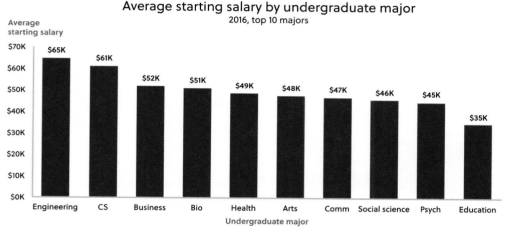

The graph title is larger than the subtitle.

Lower intensity axis labels establish a hierarchy of information.

Keep similar elements similar sizes

Keep elements of the same type the same size. If the point of this graph is the comparison between the starting salary for a business school major and the higher starting salaries of computer science and engineering graduates, resist the temptation to increase the font size of the "business" bar to focus the audience on it. Instead, keep all the category labels the same size and use strategic labeling and intensity to increase their salience.

Label and highlight strategically to focus your audience on key points

Selectively labeling is a powerful tool to focus your audience on the right comparison. Since ink draws the eye, eliminating the labels on nonessential data points focuses the audience on the key data points. Like any powerful tool, however, the consequences of misuse are high. If the audience doesn't understand the justification for focusing on these points, they are likely to suspect that you have focused them on one aspect of the comparison in order to distract them from an issue elsewhere.

To label selectively, therefore, you must share the audience's purpose for looking at this data. For this example, let's assume that the audience is the faculty of a business school where the population of undergraduate business majors has been declining. It's widely accepted that the decline is driven by students opting to study engineering and computer science instead. Since the fewer students who opt for a major, the fewer faculty a department can support, the stakes for declining enrollment are meaningful to the faculty. Assume that this graph is just one visualization within a longer conversation about potential causes.

Since this hypothetical conversation focuses on comparing the starting salaries for business majors with those of engineering and computer science majors, one could make an argument in favor of labeling just these points with the salary value they encode. Notice how the labeling and intensity choices below focus the audience on the leftmost bars.

SELECTIVE HIGHLIGHTING AND LABELING CAN FOCUS THE AUDIENCE ON THE KEY COMPARISONS

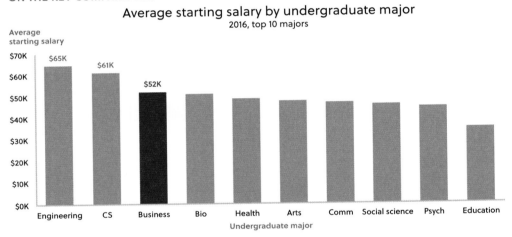

Average starting salary by undergraduate major
2016, top 10 majors

Source: Sallie Mae, from Statista.com

This choice makes sense only in the context of this specific conversation, where the audience assumes that the primary choice students are making is among the majors with the highest starting salaries. In this case, selective labeling can focus the discussion and lighten the audience's cognitive load. For audiences without this shared context, the choice looks like a deliberate attempt to distort the data. For some—perhaps faculty in the disciplines without a salary figure labeling their bar—the lack of a label might border on offensive dismissal. Make every label justify its existence, but weigh the audience and context heavily when making these choices.

One concern about selective labeling is that it removes information from the graph that the audience may want to know. The Curse of Knowledge drives some of this concern. If you've seen the graph with every point labeled, the absence of some of those labels is notable.

Another reasonable concern is misinterpretation by different audiences. The more tailored a graph is to a specific audience and conversation, the easier it will be for that audience to understand it, but the less flexible it becomes for use by other audiences. In organizations where graphs are often copied from one context and shown in another, this problem can be substantial. The graph above was not designed to support a conversation about the education department. Used in the context of that conversation, the choices here would seem strange at best and insulting at worst.

The paradox is that the graphs designed to serve multiple audiences and conversations are the most likely to be reused and misinterpreted. Graphs clearly designed for a specific explanatory purpose tend to be difficult to repurpose for other contexts. Consider this a reason to design good explanatory graphs and make sure there is an intuitive and obvious reason grounded in the audience and purpose of this graph to drive your design and labeling choices.

Add reference lines to clarify the comparison

Since graphs show relationships, all graphs are comparisons. Often you want your audience to compare the points on the graph to some standard of good or bad performance. Make sure the comparison you want the audience to make is visualized on the graph. If you don't show the audience what to compare the data to, they will compare the data to itself. Instead, use reference lines to make sure that your graph properly answers the question, "Compared to what?"

TAKE ADVANTAGE OF COMMON REFERENCE LINES AND REGIONS

Reference type	Common examples
Summary statistics	Averages (means and medians) Best-fit regression lines Confidence intervals
Targets and thresholds	Minimum acceptable service levels High/low markers Targets (lines for thresholds and areas for ranges) Trigger points (for intervention, escalation, or investigation)
Events	Before/after Notable events (e.g., large one-time orders) Notable periods (e.g., recessions)
Categories	Descriptive groupings (e.g., laggards vs. stars)

Without visualizing a comparison as a reference line or region, the implied comparison of the graph is among the data points shown. This may not be the comparison you intend to make.

GDP per capita
5 largest middle- and low-income economies, 2018

Russia	$25.5K
Mexico	
China	
Brazil	
India	$7.1K

$0K $10K $20K $30K

Source: World Bank; Adjusted for Purchasing Power Parity (PPP)

Without any other point of comparison, the implicit suggestion of the GDP graph is that the audience should compare the countries shown to each other. Only showing the numerical value of Russia's and India's GDPs draws visual attention to these points and reinforces the idea that the primary comparison here is between Russia and India. Since Russia's GDP per capita is 3.5 times larger than India's, this graph suggests that the Russian economy is robust. Adding reference lines focuses the audience on comparisons that may be more appropriate.

REFERENCE LINES CHANGE THE IMPLIED COMPARISON

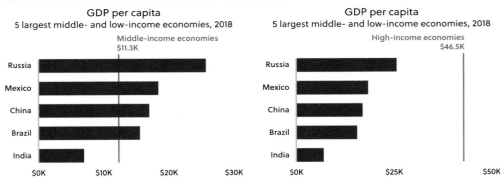

GDP per capita
5 largest middle- and low-income economies, 2018

Source: World Bank; Adjusted for Purchasing Power Parity (PPP)

The graph on the left adds a reference line for the average GDP per capita among the middle-income countries. This strengthens the perception that the Russian economy is strong. The graph on the right changes the comparison by adding a reference line for the average GDP per capita of the world's high-income countries. With a different point of reference, none of these middle- and low-income economies look so robust. The responsibility for choosing the appropriate point of comparison falls on you as the person explaining the data. One way the audience evaluates the credibility of the analysis is by evaluating the soundness of your choices.

WATCH OUT: *Good, bad, well, poorly, quickly,* and *slowly* demand points of comparison

Whenever you find yourself assigning value words to your data that imply good or bad performance, make sure that the point of comparison for that evaluation is visualized on the graph.

Any comparison between the data and some measure of what it means to do well depends on the point of comparison. Your 20% year-over-year growth might be phenomenal in a stable industry or abysmal in an industry growing 200% a year. Your slowest growing product line might still dominate its category when compared to the appropriate competitive products. Without visualizing industry growth or the appropriative competitive set, the implied comparison for the audience is the company's revenue performance compared against itself in the past, or a product's performance compared to dissimilar products your company happens to also produce.

Failing to visualize theses comparisons is a common mistake. This data can often be difficult to obtain. Reference lines are challenging to graph in some of the most common visualization tools, and the Curse of Knowledge often blinds people to the fact that they have an internalized understanding of what good or bad performance looks like. This understanding is often shared by your immediate coworkers, who may likewise fail to notice that the implicit point of comparison isn't explicitly visualized on your graph. The work of making these comparisons visually explicit is a high-yield investment of time.

Annotate to add clarity via proximity

The highest-quality visuals are self-sufficient. The audience can understand their meaning without additional verbal or written explanation outside of the graph. Annotation—text added within a visual to explain it—helps graphs meet this standard.

Effective annotation takes advantage of the Gestalt principle of proximity. Putting explanatory text near the data it explains creates less cognitive load than forcing the audience to connect a bullet point outside the graph to the relevant information within the graph. Annotation can be used to label regions, explain how the data was calculated, and help the audience see past outliers.

Annotate to label regions

The scatterplot below (left) uses a diagonal reference line to demarcate where population inflow and outflow are equal, dividing the graph into two regions. The regions are annotated with text in the opposite corners to help the audience decode which points represent states with net population increases and which represent states with net decreases. The text is the same color as the points in the region it refers to, increasing clarity through the Gestalt principle of similarity.

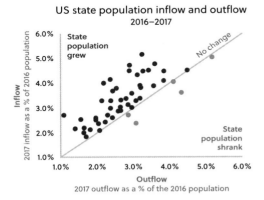

LABEL REGIONS TO CLARIFY THE KEY COMPARISON

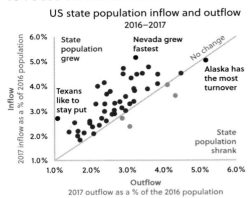

LABEL OUTLIERS TO ALLOW THE AUDIENCE TO FOCUS ON THE KEY DATA

Annotate to address outliers

We are programmed to notice differences,[5] which is why outliers and exceptions draw the eye. Use annotation to address audience questions about the exceptions on the graph so they can turn their focus back to the key point. The key intended message of the scatterplot above (right) is that the populations of most states in the US are growing. The annotations explain the outliers in order to allow the audience to return their focus to the key point. The labels here clarify the meaning of the graph, reinforcing that the states farther from the center line have the largest changes in population. Place annotations carefully. Use proximity to clarify which point they refer to, but avoid covering up other data. To avoid excess clutter, use lines to connect the annotation to the data point only when absolutely necessary.

---

[5] One evolutionary theory is that the cost of failing to notice something that ought to stand out—like the movement of a predator shaking a tree—is so dangerous that we are over-sensitive to false signals, like that same tree just rustling in the wind.

Annotate to explain the calculation

Use annotation to help explain how the data was calculated. Choosing an individual data point to explain the data is an example of using selective labeling to focus the audience on an important data point. It also takes advantage of the human inclination to extrapolate from specifics.[6] This approach helps mitigate the inherent complexity of scatterplots. Notice how annotating a single state—West Virginia—clarifies the meaning of every point, even though only one point is labeled.

**LABEL DATA POINTS TO EXPLAIN THE DATA
AND DRAW FOCUS TO KEY POINTS**

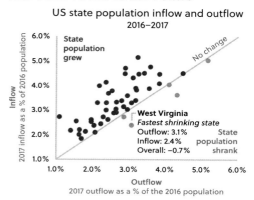

Source: US Census Bureau American Community Survey

The same annotation principle can be used with time series graphs to explain important moments of change or underlying conditions that the audience needs to know. The graph below labels both meaningful points in time as well as ranges.

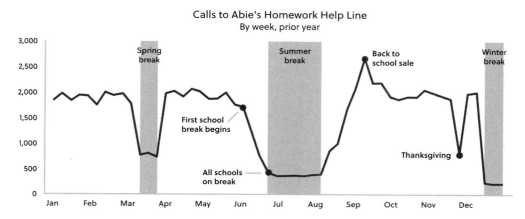

---

[6] See chapter 7, section "Concrete > abstract," for more detail.

Split two y-axis graphs

Graphs with two y-axes help explore data efficiently. They can be effective with an audience that sees data in this format regularly, but they often confuse audiences who are unfamiliar with them. Communicators who use this format often fall prey to the Curse of Knowledge, forgetting that there is no intuitive justification for what kind of data is left axis data and what kind of data is right axis data.

Two y-axis graphs are difficult for audiences to interpret.

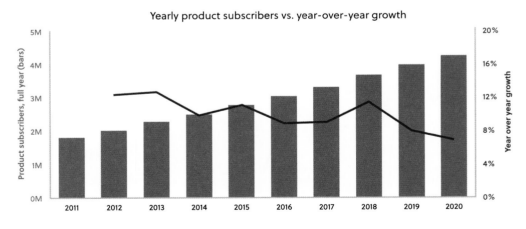

Yearly product subscribers vs. year-over-year growth

This graph of a company's subscribers and the yearly growth of that subscriber base uses a common two axis form with bars mapped to the left axis and growth mapped to the right. Even if you are used to this convention, it still takes a moment to understand how the data is related. Color coding the axes—with the text of one axis in teal and the other in burgundy—helps reduce confusion, but it still adds cognitive load for the audience.

Alternatives to these graphs keep a shared x-axis and either separate the elements vertically into two graphs or label the values of the second axis directly on the line.

SEPARATE GRAPHS TO HELP THE AUDIENCE UNDERSTAND WHAT EACH ENCODING MEANS

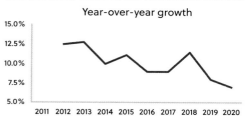

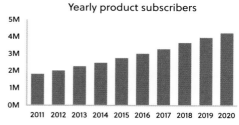

PLACE THE LINE ABOVE THE BARS TO AVOID INTERACTION AND LABEL VALUES DIRECTLY

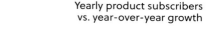

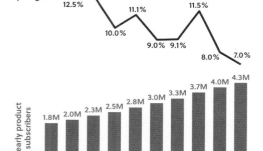

(Left) Separate graphs
- Focuses the audience on trends
- Easy to differentiate which variable each element encodes
- Requires graphs to line up precisely

(Right) Label directly
- Focuses the audience on individual values
- Best used when line variation is minimal

WATCH OUT: Make things as simple as possible, but no simpler

The overriding message of this chapter and book is to aim for simplicity whenever possible in visual design. When complexity is necessary and irreducible, consider these additional tools to help manage the cognitive load on the audience.

Display complex graphs one element at a time. One way to manage the cognitive load of a complex graph is to present it in layers, revealing one element at a time and allowing the audience to absorb each component before revealing the new one. This approach takes advantage of the Curse of Knowledge. The audience forgets what it was like before they understood each component of the graph and can turn their full processing capacity to the next chunk of information.

Show the "same" graph multiple times with different points labeled and elements highlighted. If one graph has multiple relevant points, show it multiple times with varying highlighting and annotation. Focus the audience on one point at a time, in order to convey multiple points with the same underlying visual.

Consider alternatives to slides. Slides are a poor medium for dense and complex graphs. They eliminate the context and discussion necessary to understand all their components. If the data and situation demand complexity, consider whether an alternate type of communication, like a report or a long email, would better support the complexity of the topic.

Be clear about what's in it for them. The better the audience understands how this data impacts their day-to-day lives, the more willing they will be to invest mental energy in decoding complexity. No design choice increases the audience's tolerance for cognitive load as powerfully as a compelling explanation of how this data impacts their life or livelihood.

Key concepts from this chapter

Effective graphs maximize the data–ink ratio.

THE GRAPH DESIGN CHECKLIST

Step	Test
Eliminate non-data ink	• Have you removed every element that can be removed without removing meaning? • Have you added back in any non-data ink needed to build credibility with this audience?
Maximize data ink	• Is every element labeled? • Is the text large enough that your audience will be able to read it?
Create a visual hierarchy	• Is the most important visual element on the graph the most visually salient? • Are all the comparisons visualized explicitly? • Are outliers and visually salient points annotated?

If you remember nothing else . . .

The goal is to create graphs that are perfectly transparent windows into the underlying data.

Start mentally from a blank page, and make every element of your graph justify its existence to your audience.

Design for your actual audience: regardless of what this book says, if your boss likes data shown in a certain way, format it that way for them.

Whenever you find yourself assigning value words to your data that imply good or bad performance, make sure that the point of comparison for that evaluation is visualized on the graph.

Exercise: Redraw the graph

Redraw the messy graphs below to improve them. Think about choosing the best graphical form and maximizing the data–ink ratio. Use the information provided about the audience and the context of the discussion to make choices that focus the audience on the key comparison.

Graph 1: Retail store closings

Context	A high-level presentation on the economic outlook (taking place at the end of 2017)
Audience	CFOs of large companies across a variety of industries (not just retail)
Communicator	Market forecasting company with a strong reputation and high credibility with the audience
Goal	Demonstrate to the audience that 2017 retail store closings were the highest since 2008

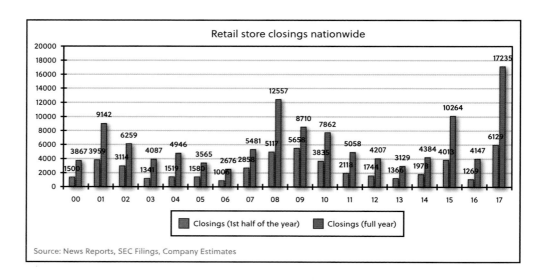

Graph 2: Power outages following Hurricanes Wilma and Irma

Context	An introductory slide as part of a longer presentation
Audience	Community leaders seeking an update on how well Florida recovered from Hurricane Wilma as compared to Irma
Communicator	A trusted representative from the US Energy Information Administration, which measures issues related to US energy infrastructure
Goal	Indicate that Hurricane Irma left more customers without power than Hurricane Wilma, but recovery from hurricane Irma has been faster

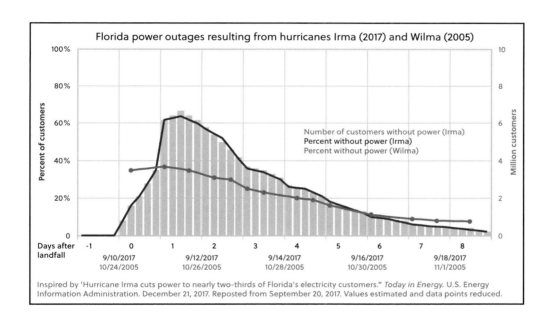

Florida power outages resulting from hurricanes Irma (2017) and Wilma (2005)

Number of customers without power (Irma)
Percent without power (Irma)
Percent without power (Wilma)

Inspired by 'Hurricane Irma cuts power to nearly two-thirds of Florida's electricity customers." *Today in Energy*. U.S. Energy Information Administration. December 21, 2017. Reposted from September 20, 2017. Values estimated and data points reduced.

Build Effective Slides

(with the point in mind)

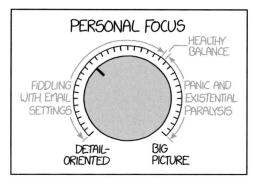

Source: https://xkcd.com/1796

Most business audiences consume graphs as slide presentations. This chapter moves from the process of building effective graphs to the process of building effective slides that present those graphs to your audience. It focuses on the most important part of slide design: identifying the point of each slide. The chapter walks you through how to write the point as the headline of your slide and offers a series of tests to help reinforce effective design choices. The exercise allows you to practice creating slides that reinforce the slide's headline.

Identify a single point for each slide

The point of the slide is the reason why you are showing this data to this audience. Help lower your audience's cognitive load by making sure that each of your slides has a single, clear point. Because humans see what is salient and only one thing can be most salient at a time, audiences can absorb only one new point at a time.

Limiting each slide to a single point helps break ideas into their most easily digestible components, lowers cognitive load, and increases your audience's ability to absorb and accept your conclusions. Trying to make multiple points in a single slide reduces the audience's ability to internalize each chunk and remember your message. If you need to make fifty points in your presentation for your audience to accept the conclusion, make a fifty-slide deck.

Write your point as a headline

The single most important thing you can do to reduce cognitive load on the audience is to write the point of the slide on the slide. The point is the most important thing the audience needs to know about this data. It should be written out in the most important position on the slide: at the top in the largest font on the page.[1]

When the words at the top of the slide explain the point of the slide, we will refer to it as the headline. You may not have heard the word headline used to refer to the text at the top of a slide, because there's no standard term for this text. In practice, you may hear it referred to as a message title, action title, header, tagline, or a tag. The term headline is used here for consistency and to reinforce the idea that this text ought to summarize the point of the slide.

Headlines clarify your thinking by forcing you to justify how every graph and slide serve the needs of the audience. Writing them focuses you on the point your audience needs to understand. It forces you to build data visualizations that clarify your point.

---

[1] There is a high degree of variation in the visual routes individual audience members take through slides, but scanning from top to bottom and left to right is a common visual path.

Good headlines pass three tests
1. They explain the point of the data shown
2. They are supported by the data shown on the graph
3. They are short enough to fit at the top of a page in a large font

Sample headlines
- Outcomes improve when a single care team supports all patients recovering from similar procedures
- Adopting a single content management system across the organization will save €3M over the next two years
- Employees say they are disengaged from their work because our processes are inefficient and frustrating

In some organizations, the headline appears at the bottom of the slide. Audiences used to seeing the point at the bottom of the slide will look for it there. They experience higher cognitive load if the point is in a different location. As a best practice, aim to present data in whatever form minimizes cognitive load on your audience. Matching the established norms in your organization will lower cognitive load more than variation for the sake of variation.

Titles are not headlines

Just because there is text at the top of a slide does not mean that slide has a headline. Authors often use the words at the top of a slide to label the graph without explaining what it means. Words that label what's being shown without explaining why it's being shown are titles, not headlines.

USE HEADLINES TO CONVEY THE POINT
USE TITLES TO LABEL THE GRAPH

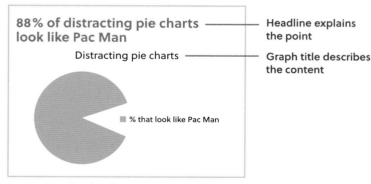

88% of distracting pie charts look like Pac Man —————— Headline explains the point

Distracting pie charts —————— Graph title describes the content

■ % that look like Pac Man

Source: Adapted from http://www.mattcutts.com/blog/pac-man-graph-in-google-chart-api/

Though most people use the terms interchangeably, headlines and titles are used here to clarify what is and is not a headline. A title identifies what is being discussed. It is not a sentence. A headline describes why that data matters to the audience and almost always has a verb in it.[2]

Compare the following title of a hypothetical article about a Nobel Prize winner with a headline on the same topic. The title identifies the topic of the article. The headline explains why the audience should care.

Title: This Year's Nobel Prize Winner

Headline: Richard Thaler receives Nobel Prize for challenging the idea that humans make rational economic choices

Titles have a home on every graph. They should be above the graph where they identify what the graph encodes. Headlines, which explain the point of showing the audience this data, belong at the top of your slides.

The table below compares a set of graph titles and the slide headlines that could emerge from them. Notice that the titles could apply to any display of that data, no matter what the data shows. The headlines describe a specific instance of that data. Titles are reusable every time you refresh the data in the graph; headlines are not.

Graph title	Slide headline
Turnover impact by scheduling option	Flexible scheduling options could reduce turnover by 8%
Sweater sales by color	Cerulean blue sweaters outsell all other colors combined
Trial period user behavior conversion rates	Users who configure their alerts during the free trial period are 3x more likely to convert to paying customers

---

[2] The distinction between headlines and titles comes from journalism where articles–like slides ought to–always have headlines, not titles. Headlines on slides also follow the news convention of ending without a period, even though they are almost always full sentences.

WATCH OUT: Wasting an audience's time is a bigger insult than explaining the data

Presenters unused to headlines fear they will generate a negative response from the audience. Some common concerns are:

If I tell them what the point of the data is, I'm biasing the audience. Shouldn't the data be allowed to speak for itself? Data cannot speak. The process of deciding which data to graph and how to visualize it requires you to make choices about what the data means. These are decisions that data cannot make on its own. Unless the audience wants to go through the exploratory process themselves, treat the invitation to share results as an invitation to help the audience think about what the data means. Trust that the audience will appreciate how the clarity of headlines accelerates their thinking, even if they disagree with the implications.

The point is obvious from the data. Won't they feel patronized if I tell them the conclusion they ought to draw? Good headlines respect the audience by shifting more of the cognitive load from the audience onto the communicator. By explaining why this data matters, headlines help speed up the process the audience is already attempting: to move from decoding the data to understanding what it means. Respect your audience by acknowledging the reality of the situation: you have a purpose for presenting this information and a reason why you think it is important. If the point is obvious, the audience will accept it and move on. Headlines focus audiences on the right test: does this data support the conclusion you have drawn? Trust that they will still investigate the data to confirm that they arrive at the same point themselves, but the whole process will move faster.

That's so many words. Doesn't it add cognitive load to the audience? Explaining the point of the data in a headline takes more words than a title uses. If you are unused to reading and writing them, headlines can feel like they add substantial cognitive load. However, the cost to the audience is lower than it appears, and the return is considerable. Humans read about 400 words per minute. Going from a 4-word title to a 10-word headline costs about one second of audience processing time. The benefit of a strong headline is that it ensures your audience knows why you are sharing this data with them. It allows them to quickly evaluate whether the data supports the point you are trying to make, and it minimizes the chance that the audience will seize upon unrelated or unimportant points.

Use headlines to clarify your graphs

Headlines help focus graphs and increase their explanatory power. The slides below—which were adapted from real situations—illustrate how identifying the point of the slide and writing it as a headline can help improve the visuals that support your point. In the examples below, the original slides had titles, but no headlines. The authors then created the revised versions in response to audience feedback. Compare the two versions. Notice how adding a headline that identifies the point of the slide inspired the authors to modify other elements on the slide.

Use headlines to focus the visual on the point

The intended audience for this slide was hospital leadership deciding which heart valve replacement procedure the organization should focus on. The Kaplan Meier survival rate estimator is used in healthcare to measure the success of an intervention. The higher the percentage, the more patients survived after the procedure. The three lines correspond to different procedures for replacing faulty heart valves.

TITLE FAILS TO PORTRAY THE POINT

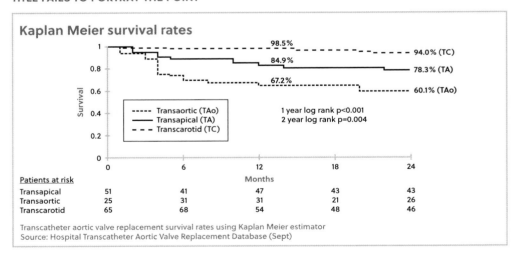

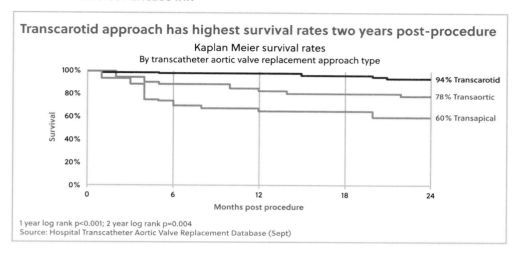

Adding a headline helped the author identify and cut excess ink

The revision lessens cognitive load by focusing the audience on the more successful procedure. The headline also helps the noncardiologists in the room understand that the key comparison here is between people's survival rates after different types of procedures.

Adding the headline helped the author better recognize the audience's needs and remove excess ink. The author removed the legend and labeled each line by procedure, focusing the audience on the point of the slide. Since the norm in this hospital was to show only statistically significant data and the point of the slide is the final survival rates, the author removed the one-year data point labels and shifted all the statistical data to the notes for those who needed it. The final slide contains almost all the same data as the original, but it is much clearer for the audience.

Use headlines to identify the correct comparison

The intended audience for this slide was the technical leadership of a company deciding whether to invest in tools that help automate the process of deploying software updates.

TITLE DOESN'T MATCH THE
COMPARISON SHOWN

HEADLINE HELPS IDENTIFY THE
RIGHT COMPARISON

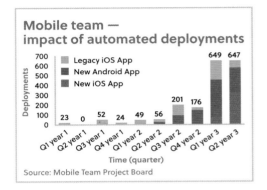

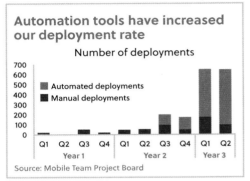

Identifying the key point helped the author identify the correct comparison

In the original graph, the Curse of Knowledge led the author to assume the audience understood that the company's new Android and iOS apps had incorporated automated deployment tools. These tools speed up the process of releasing software updates and allow organizations to update their software much more often.

Having identified the key point of the slide, the author realized that segmenting the data by app type didn't support the conversation this slide was meant to support: the value of automated software deployment tools. The revised slide segments the data by deployment type rather than the operating system of the app. The revision helped the author identify the comparison that best supported the point the author was trying to make.

Test your slides to maximize clarity and impact

With a headline that identifies the point, you can run the slide through a series of tests that maximize the clarity and impact of your data. Slides that pass all of the following tests are more likely to deliver high value for the audience while maintaining low cognitive load. For every slide you generate, make sure to ask yourself:

1. Does the slide pass the self-sufficiency test?
2. Does the slide pass the blink test?
3. Does this data support that headline?
4. Does the slide's language align?

1. Does the slide pass the self-sufficiency test?

Slides are self-sufficient when the point of the slide could be understood if either the headline or the graph were removed. A slide passes the self-sufficiency test if:[3]

1. The headline alone, without the graph, is sufficient for *this audience* to understand the point of the data.
2. The graph alone, without the headline, is sufficient for *this audience* to infer what the headline is *and believe it*.

The first self-sufficiency test builds on the headline rule. Headlines, by definition, always pass the first self-sufficiency test because they explain the point of the slide to the audience. If your headline fails the self-sufficiency test, then you've titled the slide rather than writing a proper headline.

Slides fail the second self-sufficiency test when the graph lacks enough information to support the headline. This is usually because some aspect of the comparison the author wants the audience to make is not visualized. Since all graphs are comparisons, all the elements you want the audience to compare must be visualized; otherwise, the audience will compare the data with itself.

Some common self-sufficiency failures are shown below with redrawn versions that visualize every component of the comparison the author makes in the headline.

---

[3] Kaiser Fung proposed a similar self-sufficiency test. His version asks if
- A graph still shows the correct relationship without the numerals
- The relative value of the numerals can be correctly estimated from the graph

The version used here also incorporates themes from his trifecta checklist, another excellent validation tool. Fung's blog and links to his other work can be found at https://junkcharts.typepad.com/.

Kaiser Fung, "The Self-Sufficiency Test," *Junk Charts*, October 1, 2005, https://junkcharts.typepad.com/junk_charts/2005/10/the_selfsuffici.html.

Visualize measures of comparison

The first version fails to provide sufficient measures of comparison

Neglecting to visualize comparisons of good, bad, strong, weak, fast, and slow are the most common failures of the self-sufficiency test. Without the headline, the graph on the left is insufficient for the audience to recognize that new product sales have been weak. For the graph to be self-sufficient, it needs to visualize whatever comparison the author is using to determine the success of the new product launch. With the addition of the sales projections on the right, the graph becomes sufficient for the audience to understand the point: that sales of the new product have underperformed expectations based on prior product launches.

Visualize thresholds and targets

PERFORMANCE THRESHOLD NOT VISUALIZED

This slide fails the self-sufficiency test because the graph doesn't provide enough information to support the headline.

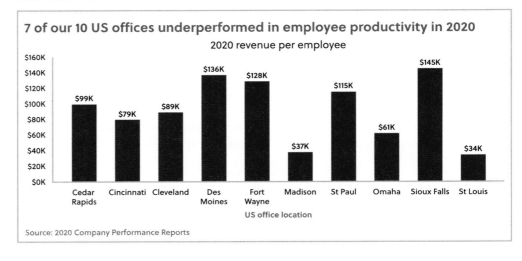

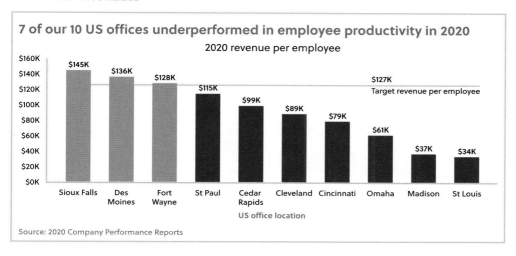

7 of our 10 US offices underperformed in employee productivity in 2020

2020 revenue per employee

Target revenue per employee

US office location

Source: 2020 Company Performance Reports

The first version doesn't show what it means to underperform

Since the audience cannot see the productivity target, the first graph is not self-sufficient. Make sure to always visualize targets and thresholds. The revision visualizes every concept in the headline by:

- Adding in a reference line to show the productivity target
- Sorting the offices based on performance to help the audience mentally group them
- Using a more intense shade for the underperforming offices to direct focus to these offices

Visualize causation hypotheses

CAUSATION NOT VISUALIZED

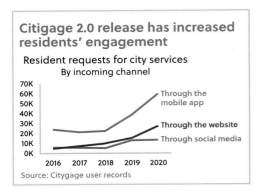

CAUSATION VISUALIZED

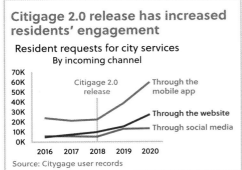

The first version is insufficient to prove the causality referenced in the headline

The original slide fails the second self-sufficiency test because the graph doesn't show the event referred to in the headline. It's insufficient to convey the message that the uptick in requests followed a new version of the software.

The second graph adds information about Citygage 2.0's release date. The upward trend following release doesn't meet academic standards for proving causality, but the author of this slide felt it was justified by other data within the presentation and would be uncontroversial for the intended audience. For a different audience, the author might need to provide additional data.

The slide could be improved by focusing on other data that better proves causation

Ideally, a randomized test could prove that the release of Citygage 2.0 caused increased engagement. If this kind of test isn't feasible, a comparison to the engagement rates in other cities still using version 1.0 could also help support the point.

2. Does the slide pass the blink test?

The next test for a powerful explanatory data visualization is the blink test (sometimes called the "glance test"). Slides that make the key comparison obvious at a quick glance, or before the viewer has time to blink, pass the test. The rewards of designing slides that pass the blink test are less obvious than the penalties for failing it.

Slides that fail the blink test lead uninvested audiences to the wrong conclusions and lead engaged audiences to challenge the messenger. If the audience doesn't trust that the message of your slide will stay the same between initial glance and closer inspection, they may doubt whether your underlying analysis will hold up under more rigorous scrutiny.

Some common blink test failures are shown below with redrawn versions that better emphasize the point.

Emphasize the comparison visually

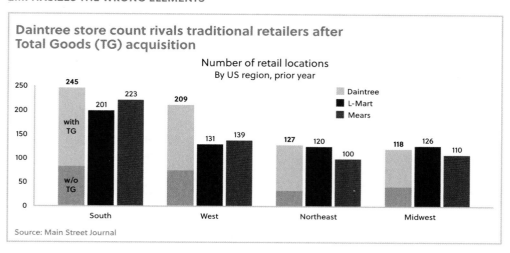

Hue focuses the audience on the comparison between L-Mart & Mears.

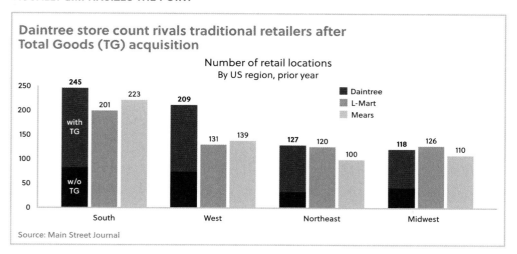

Revision uses hue to focus the audience on the intended comparison.

The graphical elements you want the audience to focus on should be the most visually prominent. The revised slide uses a higher contrast color for Daintree and a lower contrast color for the other retailers to focus the audience on the point the headline makes.

Match your language to the visuals

TRENDS MOVE THE "WRONG" WAY **CUES ESTABLISH WHICH WAY IS "GOOD"**

(Left) Audiences tend to assume down is bad.

(Right) Label which direction is "good" to help focus the audience.

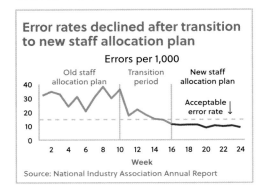

For most measures, up is good. Avoid words like "improvement" and "increased" when the graph appears to be trending downward. The revised slide better passes the blink test by changing the language in the headline to match the graph and visually indicating the desired result with a target line for the acceptable error rate.

Visualize aggregates and averages for easier comparison

NO CLEAR COMPARISON

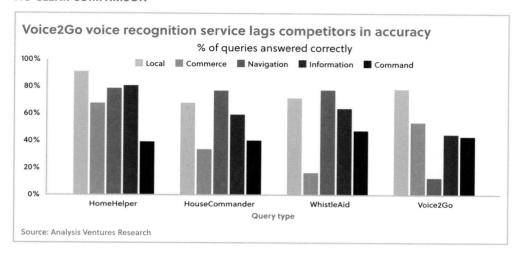

COMPARISON VISUALIZED

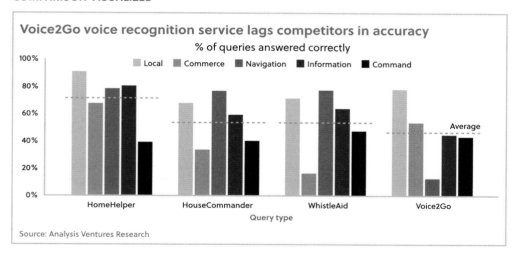

Average lines clarify the comparison.

Make sure the relationship described in the headline is visualized in the graph, so that it passes the blink test. The original graph asks the audience to compare the different voice recognition services, but it doesn't provide a clear visual comparison. It fails the blink test. The revision adds in average lines to allow easy comparison between the services, supporting the headline at a glance.

3. Does this data support that headline?

The data shown on the slide should be both necessary and sufficient to support the headline. Writing headlines that go beyond the data shown is a common slide error. Slides with headlines that propose actions often fall into this trap. These slides often show partial evidence to support the proposed action but leap over other logically required evidence straight to the suggested action.

In the following example, the headline argues that an organization should invest in more staff to submit proposals faster. The data shows that it takes this organization an average of 6.5 weeks to submit a proposal, and that the average proposal is submitted after 4.2 weeks.

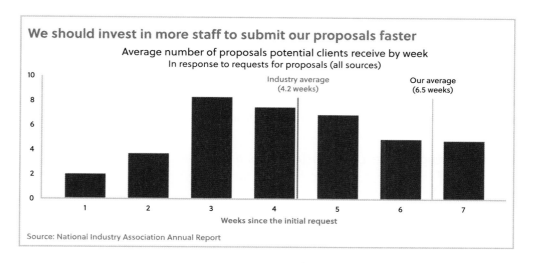

We should invest in more staff to submit our proposals faster

Average number of proposals potential clients receive by week
In response to requests for proposals (all sources)

Industry average
(4.2 weeks)

Our average
(6.5 weeks)

Weeks since the initial request

Source: National Industry Association Annual Report

The delay between this company's timing and the average suggests there are ways to shorten the response time. However, this data is insufficient to demonstrate that more people would fix the problem, or even that this is a problem. Maybe lack of staff isn't the cause of the longer than average response time. Maybe this organization wins business far more often than others because of the extra time they take to craft their proposals. It's unlikely the case for more staff can be made in a single slide. To make that case with this slide, you would need to demonstrate at least three additional things:

- More staff decreases the amount of time it takes to submit a proposal.
- Submitting proposals faster wins more business.
- Adding more staff will generate enough additional business to justify the cost.

Headlines that go beyond the data on the slide are common because they often work. When the audience and presenters share implicit assumptions, no one may notice these logical leaps. If decision-makers in this organization already believe that the team is understaffed and that faster responses would win more business, this might be the evidence that pushes them to hire more people. However, when the audience doesn't hold the same underlying assumptions as the presenter, these slides fail. In the worst case, the audience may believe the communicator leapt from one piece of evidence to the conclusion in order to hide evidence that weakens the point.

4. Does the slide's language align?

Asking the audience to do mental math or varying the language between the headline and the slide are both common errors that increase cognitive load on the audience. Avoiding repetition may be good writing advice, but it is bad slide design advice. Improve your slides by using consistent language in the headline and the graph. Make sure that any numbers that appear in the headline also appear in the graph, relieving your audience of the need to do mental arithmetic.

ORIGINAL VERSION VARIES LANGUAGE AND ASKS THE AUDIENCE TO DO MENTAL MATH

"More than half" requires audience to identify and add two segments in their heads.

The categories "medicine" and "shelter" are not used within the graph.

The word "choice" is not used within the graph.

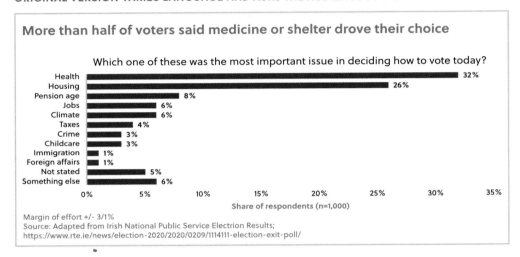

58% referenced in headline is shown on the graph.

Categories referred to in the headline match the categories shown on the graph.

The headline is framed around the "most important issue." This is the same language from the question being graphed.

Graph uses intensity to focus the audience on the point.

REVISED VERSION ALIGNS THE LANGUAGE TO REDUCE COGNITIVE LOAD

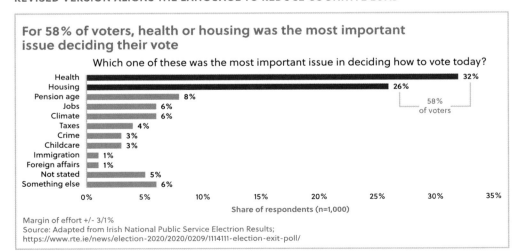

WATCH OUT: High-impact, high-clarity slides resist misuse by others

Slides can be easily misused when they are reused by others. Out of context, the conclusions other communicators draw from the same data may be different or even the opposite of what the data supports. When others shuffle your slides into their decks,[4] the process—like a game of telephone—can distort the audience's understanding of what the data shows and how it ought to be interpreted.

Slides that pass the tests here are far less likely to be misused in this way. Adapting your slides to support a different point will be difficult if your slide has a clear headline, passes the self-sufficiency test by visualizing the intended comparison explicitly, and reinforces that comparison with aligned language.

Key concepts from this chapter

Good headlines are the foundations on which effective slides are built.

THE SLIDE IMPACT CHECKLIST

Does your slide	Test your slide
Have a headline?	Does your slide explain why this audience is looking at this graph? Is there a verb in it?
Pass the self-sufficiency test?	Is this headline alone sufficient for this audience to understand your point? Is this graph alone sufficient for your audience to infer the headline and believe it?
Pass the blink test?	Does this graph suggest at a quick glance the point it is trying to convey? Is the message suggested at first glance the same message suggested by the graph on closer inspection?
Support your headline?	Is the data shown on the slide necessary and sufficient for the audience to accept this headline if they accept the data?
Use aligned language?	Does the language used in the headline align with the language in the graph? Is every number referenced in the headline visible on the graph without the audience having to do any mental arithmetic?

---

[4] The consensus view seems to be that a set of slides is described as a "deck" because of its similarity to a deck of playing cards. The term appears to have originated during the time before personal computers when slides were physical pieces of 35mm film displayed on slide projectors. These slides more obviously resembled cards, and the trays that held them were called slide decks.

If you remember nothing else . . .

The single most important thing you can do to reduce the audience's cognitive load is to write a headline for every slide that explains why this audience should care.

Pass the blink test.

If the audience doesn't trust that the message of your slide will stay the same between initial glance and closer inspection, they may doubt whether your underlying analysis will hold up under more rigorous scrutiny.

Avoiding repetition may be good writing advice, but it is bad slide design advice.

Exercise: Sketch the right slide for this headline

Sharpen your skills by sketching a slide to support each of the headlines below. Include all the elements each slide would need to pass the self-sufficiency test and the blink test. Make sure the data supports the headline and that all the language is aligned.

Headlines	Sketch a slide that supports the headline
648 work hours were lost last year due to accidents, more than those lost due to all other causes combined	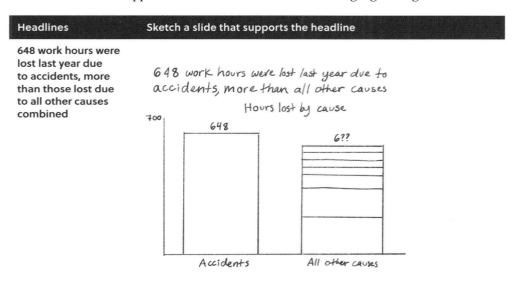
Repeat customers drive the majority of inbound customer support calls	

Headlines	Sketch a slide that supports the headline
Employees who have worked here longer do not close a higher percentage of deals	
Wall Street Journal profile drove an increase in website traffic, but no increase in sales	
Adding the phrase "#6 will blow your mind" increased Facebook ad clickthrough rates by 24%	

Part III

Organizing Your Data

—

How to arrange data into
compelling communications

CHAPTER 6

Structure Your Data

(so others can follow it)

Source: https://xkcd.com/1901

Clear communications build on clear, logical foundations. Part III shifts our focus from creating effective data visualizations to the skills required to assemble those visuals into compelling communications. This chapter introduces the Minto pyramid as a tool to organize your thoughts. It shows how to structure your thinking with a pyramid outline in order to strengthen the clarity of your communications, how to use a story to identify your main idea, and how to test the logical rigor of your arguments. The final section demonstrates how a Minto pyramid easily converts into a wide variety of communications. The exercise challenges you to structure a compelling argument based on a business case and the needs of your audience.

Begin with your ending in mind

Creating effective explanatory data visualizations requires you to shake off the Curse of Knowledge and rethink your approach from the audience's point of view. Creating complete communications that explain analytical results requires an equally dramatic shift in mindset. It requires a shift in focus from creating effective individual slides to creating a structure for your entire conversation that maximizes clarity for the audience. To revisit an analogy from chapter 1, effective communications chart a course straight to the analytical gold the audience cares about. They avoid narrating the audience through all the work you did to get there.

The foundation of any effective communication is its structure. Investing time early in the process to think through the structure of your final communication will generate more compelling analysis that is easier for audiences to accept and requires less wasted work. A solid structural foundation allows you to adapt your content quickly to almost any communication situation, whether you are generating a document, a presentation, or even a casual conversation.

This chapter introduces the Minto pyramid as a tool to facilitate any type of structured communication and explains:

- How to use a story to identify your main idea
- How to build a Minto pyramid from your main idea
- How to structure your points to minimize cognitive load
- How to support your points with logical reasoning
- How to convert your Minto pyramid into a variety of communications

Structure your communication with a Minto pyramid

Minto pyramids are a tool to organize your thinking with the final communication in mind. Named after Barbara Minto, who popularized their use, they organize communications around what the audience needs to know and the evidence they need to accept your point.[1]

The pyramid approach visualizes the outline of your communication as a two-dimensional, branching tree. These trees are sometimes called idea trees, idea charts, branching outlines, or just Mintos. At the top of the tree is the main idea of your communication: whatever you want the audience to understand, believe, or do as a result of this communication.

MINTO PYRAMIDS OUTLINE YOUR ARGUMENT AS A BRANCHING TREE

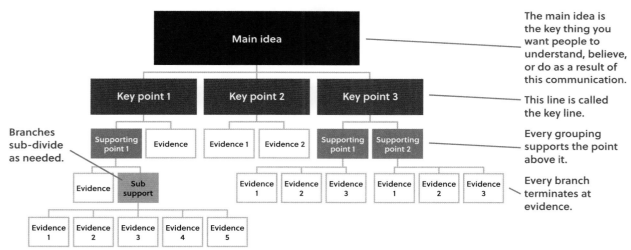

Supporting the main idea is a group of boxes with your key points. Barbara Minto calls this critical group your key line. Each point in the key line provides one idea that supports the main idea above it. Taken together, the key points should be the ideas your audience needs to believe in order to accept your main idea. In other words, if an audience accepts all your key points, they should be ready to accept your main idea.

---

[1] Barbara Minto built out the concept of the pyramid while at the consulting firm McKinsey & Company. She popularized it in her book *The Pyramid Principle* and over decades of workshops. Her approach has been widely adopted by professional services firms where communicating analytical results is the core of their business. This chapter owes an enormous debt to Barbara Minto personally and to the decades of field testing her approach has undergone.

Barbara Minto suggests thinking of every level within the pyramid as a series of questions and answers, with each box provoking a question answered by the boxes below it. Use this question-and-answer dialogue to work from your conclusion down to the evidence needed to support each assertion.

STRUCTURE YOUR PYRAMID AS A SERIES OF QUESTIONS AND ANSWERS

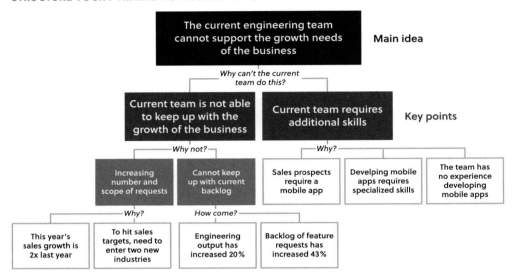

Minto pyramids can go as many levels deep as needed, with each box providing an answer to the question provoked by the point above it, and every box summarizing all the points directly below it. The lowest row of boxes provides the evidence that supports your chain of reasoning.

Though a Minto pyramid can go as deep as needed, no grouping should go too wide. Since the brain groups information into chunks and can only hold about three or four chunks at any given time, use the pyramid structure to chunk points into groups with a reasonable number of ideas. Aim to work deep rather than broad. Think of every box as a hook the audience can use to pull up the next level of ideas below it all the way down to your evidence. This depth allows Minto pyramids to explain how complex ideas emerge from observed evidence. They force you to show every step in your reasoning process, from evidence to the overall conclusion.

Build a pyramid even before you start your analysis

Minto pyramids are outlines. Just as outlining a term paper early in the research process helps organize your thinking and focus your research, structuring your problem as a branching tree has value at the earliest stages of the analytical process. Consider using the pyramid structure as a way to break down the problem and structure your analysis.[2]

When building a pyramid before the analysis, think of it as a set of hypotheses that your data and analysis will validate or invalidate. Just as scientific hypotheses make assumptions about outcomes in order to clarify which experiments might falsify them, making assumptions about what the data is likely to show can help you identify the analysis that will most efficiently validate or invalidate those hypotheses. Use that clarity to focus your time and analytical energy. Then, revise your pyramid based on your findings just as good scientists revise their thinking based on experimental outcomes.

The starting point of a useful analytical process is the same as a useful Minto pyramid: understanding what question your analysis answers and why this question matters to your audience.[3] The answer to that question drives the structure of your pyramid, and the path to that question is paved by the story of why this analysis exists.

Start with a story to identify the right main idea

Those trained in rigorous data analysis or scientific inquiry often have a complicated relationship with the idea of stories. For many, the word itself is tied to the concept of fiction and therefore the opposite of facts. But stories can also be true, and they are one of the most powerful ways humans organize, transmit, and retain information.

While there are many definitions of stories, one of the simplest is that stories present a causal chain of events with a beginning, middle, and end. Well-trained analysts know that establishing proper causation requires rigorous analysis, and that the real world often lacks clear beginnings, middles, and ends. Still, every analysis has at least one story in it: the story of why this analysis exists and is worthy of the audience's attention.

In creating your Minto, you need to be able to explain to the audience how you arrived at the need for this analysis. That process was a narrative journey for you, and your audience also needs a clear narrative to understand why they should devote their precious mental energy to the cognitively demanding task of absorbing your logical argument.

---

[2] Barbara Minto does not endorse using the pyramid approach this early in the process. She suggests a variety of problem-solving approaches, many of which also use a branching tree structure, but separates the analytical process from the communications process. Since the branching tree structure is such a powerful way to clarify one's thinking, I have seen it used effectively quite early in the problem-solving process, especially when you have some insight into the structure of the problem. For simplicity, and with apologies to Barbara Minto, I have used the term Minto throughout this text to refer to branching trees of any form, whether or not they plan the communication that results from an analysis.

[3] See chapter 7 for a more detailed discussion of how you can identify the WIIFT (What's In It For Them) for your audience.

Creating this story is also a critical step in your analytical process, because it verifies that your analysis resolves a problem the audience cares about. It helps generate the main idea of your Minto and dictates the structure of the communication that emerges from that main idea. This story also becomes the introduction of your communication.

In *DataStory*, presentation expert Nancy Duarte presents a simplified version of Barbara Minto's original approach to generating these introductory stories that frames the process as a three-act story with a situation, complication, and resolution representing the story's beginning, middle, and end.[4]

Like all good frameworks, this design adapts to a wide variety of circumstances once you understand its components.

- **The situation** is the context from which this analysis emerges. It is the set of uncontroversial facts that everyone agrees to.
- **The complication** explains why this situation demanded someone's attention and thinking. It often addresses what has changed or why deeper investigation is needed. It is the dramatic conflict that set this story in motion, the source of tension that was significant enough to motivate someone to create this analysis and subsequent communication.
- **The resolution** to the story is the main idea of your Minto pyramid. It is the answer or course of action that resolves the complication. It allows the main idea of your findings to bring this story to a satisfying close and engages the audience's interest in the analytical results that follow.

While these kinds of stories may not lend themselves to the kind of drama we expect from good fiction, they can still engage audiences in even the most prosaic analytical results.

THE SITUATION AND ITS COMPLICATION RESOLVE IN THE MAIN IDEA

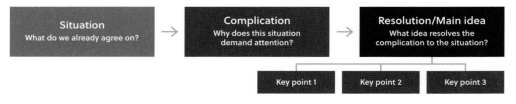

---

[4] Barbara Minto's original approach also includes a situation and complication, but breaks the resolution into a question step and an answer step. I've presented Duarte's streamlined version here because I think the increased simplicity is worth some loss of nuance, but that loss is real. Consult Minto's *The Pyramid Principle* for more detail.

The situation

The analytical process begins with understanding the situation. Just as in any story, you should think through the setting, the protagonist—the primary character—and the issue that will eventually set the story in motion. With analytical results, the setting is typically the topic that this analysis addresses. The protagonist in most business communications is the audience themselves, faced with the issue that drives this particular story: a decision they need to make, an opportunity they ought to understand, or an explanation that helps better explain the complex world they face. The facts outlined in the situation introduce the story.

When communicating your results, think of the situation as the time for the audience to reload the context they already know into their heads. By the end of the situation, the entire audience should be at the same starting position so that they can proceed through the story together. The situation may be as simple or as complex as required, but you should avoid introducing new information. The situation should only include information the audience either already knows or can easily agree with. This might be facts about which everyone is aware or a view of the world that is thoroughly uncontroversial. If the audience does not agree to critical facts, then your analysis needs to address those facts. The situation is the part that everyone should be able to agree to. It is not the place to introduce new information.

Sample Situations
Our last major facilities renovation was in 1998.
Our top five customers represent 46% of our revenue.
Engineering is currently funded through the four different departments that it serves.
We expect to hire and onboard 150 new employees at this facility this year.

The complication

In the language of narrative fiction, the complication is the inciting incident. It is not a complication in the sense that it adds complexity to the situation, nor is it a conflict in the sense that it requires two people to disagree. Instead, it is the reason why this situation demands attention, and why your analysis exists.

The complication could be driven by new information, shifting opinions, or a decision that needs to be made. The complication introduces the tension that your main idea and analysis will resolve. When presenting the complication, the degree to which the audience believes this complication introduces a problem worth solving is the degree to which they will be willing to invest in understanding your analysis.

SAMPLE SITUATIONS AND COMPLICATIONS

Situation	Complication
Online sales represent 30% of our total sales. All those sales are through ecommerce retailers.	We cannot market our upcoming product launch directly to any customers who buy our product online.
It's the end of the quarter.	At the end of every quarter, we review the performance of each member of the sales team.
We have three major investment opportunities that could each drive substantial growth in the business.	We only have the resources to invest in two of them.
Last year we introduced a mentoring program to increase employee satisfaction and reduce turnover.	The program has increased employee satisfaction by 20%, but has not had any statistically significant impact on turnover.

The resolution

The resolution resolves the dramatic tension introduced by the complication and becomes the main idea of your Minto Pyramid. This resolution may not resolve the discussion. The audience may still have to make a difficult choice or talk about an unpleasant business reality, but the resolution resolves the conflict between the situation and the complication. It completes the story of why this analysis exists and why the information you present demands the audience's attention. When delivering your results, it connects your introduction to the main body of the communication you have structured with your Minto pyramid.[5]

---

[5] Minto separates the resolution step into two steps: a question and an answer. The question is the question implied by the complication, and the answer to that question is the main idea of your Pyramid. I have elided these steps as Duarte has for simplicity, but it is useful to break them apart if you are having difficulty identifying the resolution or communicating it to others.

Situation	Complication	Resolution (pyramid main idea)
The city contracts with outside firms to cook and deliver meals to the elderly.	All of our contractors have lost money in the last four years, and half are facing bankruptcy.	We need to restructure our contracts to adjust for costs that contractors cannot control so that we will continue to be able to offer this program.
Our average time to develop a new product is 4.5 years.	We were first to market on 45% of our product launches over the past five years. In the prior five years, we were first to market 85% of the time.	We should invest to create a global, centralized data sharing system and processes to accelerate product development time.
Our CEO has set a target of 3% growth in customer volume this year. This is double the growth of the past two years.	Supporting 3% growth at current staffing ratios would require a 10% increase in head count.	Investing in improved scheduling systems would increase throughput enough to support 3% growth without increasing staffing levels.
Auditors require visual inspection of our inventory to certify our financial statements.	A global pandemic has required us to limit outside access to our facilities.	With a high-resolution helmet-mounted camera, a single team member can allow auditors to conduct a remote, real-time inventory audit.

Resolutions that are both surprising and inevitable are the hallmark of good storytelling. When the protagonist in your favorite film makes a choice that surprises you but feels like the only reasonable choice for that character, you are watching a well-crafted story. When the main idea of your analysis feels like the inevitable result of the situation and complication facing the audience, you have created an effective story too.

Support your main idea with the key points

The resolution to the introduction is the main idea of your communication. It is also the top box of your Minto pyramid and the most important idea in your communication. It explains what unites all the other ideas in a communication. With a clear main idea, you can build your Minto from the top down. If the main idea is unclear, you may need to approach your Minto from the bottom up.

Regardless of the approach you use, expect the outlining process to surface additional analytical work. The process of creating a Minto is the process of identifying the information that will be most useful to the audience, not the analysis you have readily available. Often you will discover that one difficult, time-consuming piece of analysis will be more compelling than a dozen data points to which you have easy access.

Similarly, analyses that rely on uncertain assumptions, like sales projections, may be more useful to an audience than more robust measures of past performance. Business leaders must make decisions about the future based on the best information available. Use the Minto to identify the analysis that will be the most useful to your audience and aim to make it as robust as possible. Use it to allocate your most precious resource: your time.

Build top down when the main idea is clear

With a clear main idea, you can build a Minto from the top down. The top-down approach begins with the main idea you want the audience to understand, believe, or do as a result of this communication. Ask yourself what your audience would need to believe in order to accept this main idea, and make those ideas your key points.

Each point should generate a set of additional questions that the next level of points answers. Eventually, every branch of the Minto should terminate in evidence. Use this structure to push down to the evidence your audience needs to accept your main idea.

Though it can be uncomfortable, always try to start your Minto from the top down. Working top down forces you to think through your analysis in the way that the audience will absorb it, from the main idea down to the details. You may find places where you haven't yet collected the evidence needed to support a critical idea. This approach helps you identify which pieces of evidence you need to support your argument so you can focus your time on what matters. As you gather new information along the way, this approach will help you recognize which pieces of evidence require you to change your conclusion and which are just incidental.

Build bottom up when starting from unrelated data

When you have plenty of data but lack a unifying idea about what it implies for your audience, you may need to use the bottom-up approach. Start by grouping related pieces of evidence together, and look for relationships that emerge. For example, grouping evidence about the demographics of your customers and your current market approach may suggest a better way to target your advertising.

One danger to watch out for is the temptation to think of the process like a jigsaw puzzle where you must find a place for every piece of data. Think of it more like panning for precious metals. Your job is to sift away the less valuable pieces of information until only the gold remains.

The bottom-up approach tends to be far more challenging than top-down, because it requires you to identify how apparently unrelated pieces of data fit together. It tends to be less efficient because there's no obvious place to start from, and it tends to be less effective because it doesn't begin with a topic you know your audience cares about.

When confronted with a bottom-up situation, consider converting it to a top-down approach. Revisit the situation, complication, and resolution to help identify a problem the audience cares about. Use that process to formulate a preliminary main idea and then try to work from the top down.

Seek feedback from others to refine your thinking

The most effective weapon against the Curse of Knowledge is the minds of others. Soliciting their feedback can help you identify gaps in your own thinking. The examples below walk through how two such conversions helped refine draft Minto pyramids.[6]

GETTING CLEAR ON THE PROBLEM

In this first example, the author worked in the networking support group of an IT division at a large, multi-facility technology company. The situation was that the author's group was responsible for maintaining the internet connectivity across the company's facilities. The complication was that the group was receiving an increasing number of complaints about connectivity. The author's initial Minto argued that the company ought to invest in a newer networking technology. The weaknesses of the current technology and the strengths of the new technology were the author's key points.

The main idea is generic. "Better" can be defined hundreds of ways.

There is insufficient evidence to prove that one technology is "better" than another.

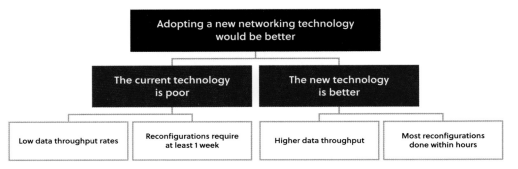

When the author solicited feedback, peers pointed out two issues that undermined the strength of the argument. They felt that:

- The main idea was generic. "Better" could be defined by many different qualities.
- The evidence was insufficient to support the key points. Throughput and configurability may be important network technology qualities, but peers didn't feel they provided enough support to show an audience that the newer technology was better than the existing one.

---

[6] The examples that follow in this and future chapters are drawn from real situations provided by working professionals in the author's classes. The peers referred to here are typically classmates who worked for different organizations in different roles but shared a similar level of work experience. In addition to removing identifying information, obscuring proprietary data, and simplifying some technical details, I have lightly fictionalized the iteration process for clarity.

Based on this feedback, the author reorganized the Minto around throughput and configurability. This allowed the author to sharpen the main idea.

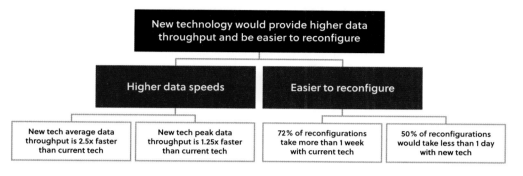

The main idea repeats both key points rather than synthesizing a single main idea.

Peers said the revision clarified the comparison. Assuming there was strong evidence to support the author's claims, this version convinced peers that the new technology was indeed faster and more configurable. The main idea, however, failed to synthesize the two key points together. Peers said that it made them wonder why the author addressed only these two qualities. They suspected that the author focused on these qualities to obscure weaknesses in other aspects of the newer technology.

Based on this feedback, the author reflected on the situation and complication that sparked the analysis. Users were complaining they could not get reliable, high-speed network access throughout the company's facilities. Root cause analysis identified two primary sources of users' complaints. The throughput of the network wasn't fast enough to support typical daily use in many facilities. In other facilities, the throughput was adequate most of the time, but high-demand events, like large meetings, caused bottlenecks that slowed the network down. Relieving these bottlenecks required reconfiguring the network in high-demand locations, a process that usually took over a week with current technology. The author realized that the resolution to this situation and complication needed to focus on user complaints. That clarity helped refine the final version of the Minto.

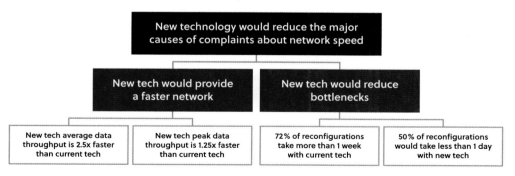

The main idea explains what separates these ideas from all others.

The key points are reworded to support the main idea more clearly.

Though this pyramid wasn't enough evidence to prove that the company ought to invest in a new network technology, it focused the audience on the problem the author wanted to discuss. Peers agreed that this main idea both explained why they should care about this topic and why it addressed these two issues exclusively.

By clarifying the situation and complication, the author was able to identify the main idea that resolved them. That clear main idea helped shape the structure of the discussion and explain why these key points were the right ones to focus on rather than all the other qualities of networking technology.

GETTING CLEAR ON THE BENEFITS OF THE SOLUTION

The argument below walks through a different author's process to identify the main idea. The situation was that the author's company helps individuals with chronic conditions like diabetes manage their diseases. Insurers pay for this service because patients with well-managed conditions need fewer high-cost medical interventions. Most patients currently register for the program via paper enrollment forms when they begin a new job. The author wants the organization to push more people to enroll online. The initial Minto combined a variety of arguments, evidence, and background information.

The main idea fails to synthesize ideas into a single main idea.

The first piece of evidence doesn't address an effect of the change.

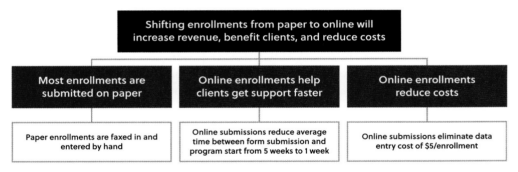

Peers noticed that the first key point didn't feel similar to the other two. It provided context about the problem, but it didn't address an effect of adopting the proposed solution. The author realized that this information was actually part of the situation that generated this proposal. With that realization, the author realized that the complication here was that online enrollment was much faster. Patients who enrolled online began receiving services an average of four weeks before patients who enrolled on paper. As a result, the company received an additional four weeks of revenue from the insurance company for these patients.

Based on this feedback, the author realized that the resolution between the situation and complication—the main idea of this argument—was that shifting more patients to online enrollment increased profit. Again, getting clear on the situation and complication helped the author identify a single main idea that focused the audience on the issue they cared about and simplified the communication.

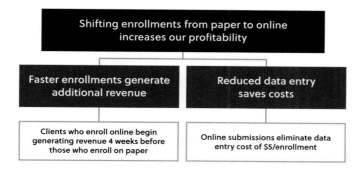

Note than in both of the preceding scenarios, much of the confusion stemmed from a lack of clarity about the main idea. The odds of this happening will be much reduced if you have properly framed the situation and complication in order to generate a compelling resolution that can serve as your main idea. It is why you should always start with the introductory story. While new information in the analytical process and conversations with others may shift your thinking, clarity about the question you are asking is typically the shortest path to the answers you seek.

Do the thinking for the audience

Effective communicators shift cognitive load from the audience onto themselves. They explain what the points mean and how they relate to each other. They don't just cherry-pick the evidence that supports their point; they address the data that appears to undermine it, too. In particular, they:

- Avoid intellectually blank ideas.
- Confront nonsupporting evidence.

AVOID INTELLECTUALLY BLANK IDEAS

Lazy points don't say anything about what binds the points below them together. Barbara Minto calls these kinds of ideas "intellectually blank." "Our analysis yields three key findings" is an intellectually blank idea. It indicates that the author has prioritized some findings above others but has failed to think through what separates those findings from all others. Effective points don't just identify the topic that groups the points below them together; they summarize what that grouping implies. Lazy main ideas are especially damaging to your persuasive power because every other idea in your analysis and communication flows from the main idea.

Intellectually blank main idea	Main idea synthesizes the key points
We have conducted manufacturing reliability tests.	The proposed manufacturing process meets all internal reliability requirements.
There are several causes of sales decline.	Production issues only explain 1/3 of the revenue declines.
We should pay attention to investments competitors are making.	To keep up with key competitors, we will need to build an advanced analytics team over the next five years.
There are risks in the outsourcing plan.	If error rates and turnaround times are 10% greater than projected, the cost benefits of outsourcing are erased.

CONFRONT NONSUPPORTING EVIDENCE

Real-world data is messy. Different pieces of evidence may imply contradictory conclusions, and the same evidence is often open to different interpretations. To convince an audience to accept your ideas, you must address their concerns. The Minto pyramid approach accommodates nonsupporting data and counterarguments to your point, but it requires you to explain why they fail to undermine your conclusion. This requirement strengthens your argument and deepens your thinking. Reframe nonsupporting data around why your conclusion still holds.

Challenge to your conclusion	Reframed as a support for the conclusion (each would need to be supported by evidence)
"Your proposal is too expensive."	The cost of this proposal is worth the investment.
"A competitor does this better already."	We can beat the competition.
"Your analysis doesn't account for [a specific factor]."	Taken together, all other factors account for only 2% of the total variation observed.
"Why haven't you considered [my favorite issue]?"	[Your favorite issue] would have to be 3x larger than any realistic scenario for it to change this conclusion.
"Didn't we try this last year and fail?"	This strategy takes advantage of important changes in the market from last year.

Maximize the impact of all your points

The layout of a Minto pyramid helps ensure that you have maintained a consistent relationship between the points within each grouping and that each grouping provides adequate evidence for the higher-level point it supports. This consistency strengthens the quality and clarity of your communication. Make sure the points within every grouping in your Minto pyramid outline are:

- Grammatically and conceptually parallel
- Ordered meaningfully
- Mutually exclusive and collectively exhaustive
- Supported by necessary and sufficient evidence

Make groupings grammatically and conceptually parallel

Points are parallel when they all share the same relationship with the idea above them in the Minto pyramid. They do this by all addressing the same question posed by the higher-level point, answering it in the same grammatical form, and being all of the same logical type. Lack of parallelism signals gaps in the underlying logic. Keep all points within a group parallel to reduce the cognitive load required to understand the relationship between your ideas. The examples that follow show errors in parallelism and potential ways to correct them.

Grammatical parallelism

Points are grammatically parallel when they answer the question implied by the idea above them in the same grammatical form. With some practice, you will find that errors in grammatical parallelism start to jump out. The examples that follow on the left fail the test of grammatical parallelism. Test them using the question-and-answer method described in the top-down approach to creating your Minto pyramid. If every point within a group completes the same answer stem, the points are grammatically parallel and likely on their way to being conceptually parallel as well.

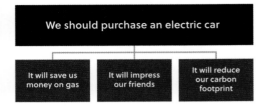

NOT GRAMMATICALLY PARALLEL

We should purchase an electric car

It will save us money on gas | It will impress our friends | Shared goal to reduce carbon emissions

Not a sentence

The third point does not complete the answer stem that begins "We should purchase an electric car because . . ." Rewrite it to mirror the grammar of the other two points.

GRAMMATICALLY PARALLEL

We should purchase an electric car

It will save us money on gas | It will impress our friends | It will reduce our carbon footprint

All three points are grammatically parallel. All begin with "it will," express some benefit, and complete an unstated answer stem that begins with "We should purchase an electric car because . . ."

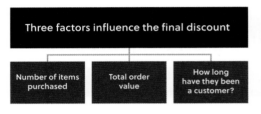

NOT GRAMMATICALLY PARALLEL

Three factors influence the final discount

Number of items purchased | Total order value | How long have they been a customer?

None of the points are grammatically parallel. Rewrite them to answer exactly the same answer stem.

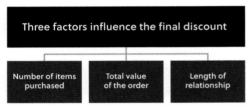

GRAMMATICALLY PARALLEL

Three factors influence the final discount

Number of items purchased | Total value of the order | Length of relationship

All three points complete the answer stem "The discount is calculated based on the . . ."

Conceptual parallelism

Conceptually parallel points all share the same logical relationship with the box above them. They are all of the same logical type. For example, if the first point in a grouping line describes the impact of a new process, all the other points in that grouping should also describe impacts of that process. If some points in the grouping described impacts and others described steps in the process, the ideas in the grouping would not be conceptually parallel.

Groupings can comprise any kind of idea, but all the ideas in a grouping must be the same type of idea. Barbara Minto suggests testing conceptual parallelism by making sure all the ideas in a group can be described with the same plural noun such as *causes, findings, reasons,* or *problems.*

Errors in conceptual parallelism can be more subtle than errors in grammatical parallelism, so use grammatical parallelism as the first test for conceptual parallelism. However, even when the points appear grammatically parallel, they may still lack a common logical relationship with the point above them. The following examples show errors in conceptual parallelism that are less grammatically obvious.

Describes methodology

Answer the question "What did the investigation find?"

The main idea suggests each box should address the findings of the investigation. The first box discusses the methodology used, not the findings. Focus on the findings to make the Minto conceptually parallel.

CONCEPTUALLY PARALLEL

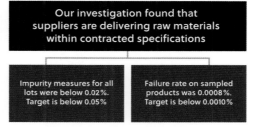

Conceptually parallel. Both answer the question "What did the investigation find?"

Both points address the findings of the investigation. Use Minto pyramids to organize the logic and evidence that supports your main point.

NOT CONCEPTUALLY PARALLEL

The primary causes of delivery delays are

| Unexpected traffic congestion | Delivery to the wrong address | 20% of drivers involved in 70% of delays |

Both provide significant causes for delivery delays

Not a cause of delivery delays

The third point is relevant to the topic, but it does not answer the question "What are the causes of delivery delays?" Investigate nonparallel points for opportunities to deepen your analysis and illuminate the true underlying causation.

CONCEPTUALLY PARALLEL

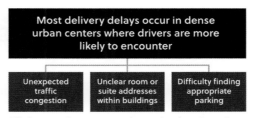

All three points answer the revised main point and provide causes of delivery delays.

Deeper investigation into the drivers with a high number of delays revealed that all worked in urban centers. Searching for a conceptually parallel structure revealed an underlying cause that better explains the data and suggests a more focused course of action.

NOT CONCEPTUALLY PARALLEL

We should create a fund to offer short-term loans to customers facing temporary financial hardship

Each year, 5% of customers face temporary financial hardships	Insufficient bank loans available	No programs outside of bank loans to address these issues
Discusses the nature of the problem	Comments on lack of alternatives	

Lack of grammatical parallelism signals a deeper conceptual problem: taken together, these three points only address the existence of a problem. These points are actually the situation and complication that led to this recommendation.

CONCEPTUALLY PARALLEL

We should create a fund to offer short-term loans to customers facing temporary financial hardship

We lose long-term revenue from valuable customers due to temporary hardships	Existing lenders show no interest in addressing this need	A short-term loan fund recovers this revenue and generates superior returns
Explains why this is a problem for us	Explains why lenders won't address this	Explains why this solution is valuable to us

Every point answers the question "Why should we create this fund?" Taken together, if true, they demonstrate that the problem exists and that solving it would generate value for us.

Order groupings meaningfully

Choose a meaningful, intuitive order for the points within a group. Order discussions about events over time or as steps in a process based on the order in which they occur. In all other cases, order the points by importance.

ORDER GROUPINGS MEANINGFULLY

Ordered by time

Customers become more valuable the longer they have been subscribers

Customers' 1st year spending just barely covers the cost of acquisition	In years 1-10, spending increases 2% per year	After year 10 spending increases 5% per year, driven by upsell offers

Ordered by process

Most breakage occurs in the packing process

35% of breakage occurs when tubes are boxed	45% of breakage occurs when boxes are assembled into pallets	20% of breakage occurs in transit

Ordered by importance

The survey found three levers we can use to increase employee satisfaction

Increasing salaries	Guaranteeing reliable work schedules	Providing clear career advancement paths

When ordering points by importance, generally order your points from most important to least important. Starting with the most important point focuses your audience on the most important issue when they have the most attention. It increases the chances that the most important issues get adequate time for discussion before the meeting ends, key people leave, or your audience starts checking messages. It respects your audience's time.

While starting with the least important point and building to the most important has the potential to add drama, few business audiences will give you the sustained focus required for this approach to work. Save your most important point for last only when the audience will have such a strong reaction to it that they will emotionally disengage.[7]

Make groupings mutually exclusive and collectively exhaustive (MECE)

In the highest-quality communications, every group of points is both mutually exclusive and collectively exhaustive, or MECE.[8] Mutually exclusive points can be evaluated entirely based on the evidence supporting them, independent of the other points in the pyramid. They do not require evidence supporting other points for the audience to understand them.

Collectively exhaustive points cover the entire universe of options related to the point above them without leaving anything out. The key to generating collectively exhaustive Minto pyramids that don't have hundreds of boxes is to have a well-formed main idea. A strong main idea is focused. It clarifies the boundary of the problem this communication addresses and describes what unites all the points below it.

Mutually exclusive

Communications fail the test of mutual exclusivity when the points overlap. Breaking down any problem into mutually exclusive segments is one of the most intellectually challenging parts of designing good analyses and good communication. After that, subdividing issues into independent components makes them both easier to understand and easier to solve. In doing so, you shift a major cognitive burden off the audience by taking it on yourself.

---

[7] This book assumes you are addressing an audience who values efficient communication—as most Western business audiences do most of the time. Of course, exceptions abound. Some situations may call for a focus on harmony or on codifying decisions already made. When the audience is very large, the focus often shifts from discussing analytical results to motivating behavior change. Consider other approaches when efficiency isn't the priority, ordering the most important point first would seem unnecessarily antagonistic, or the focus is not on the data.

[8] Most people pronounce this acronym "me-see." Barbara Minto says the proper pronunciation is a single syllable that rhymes with "piece." Barbara Minto, "MECE: I Invented It, So I Get to Say How to Pronounce It," *McKinsey Alumni Center*, May 3, 2018.

We should expand our retail banking operations to countries X, Y, & Z					
All three have low penetration rates for retail banking	All three provide opportunities for growth	We are not suited to operate outside of our region	Other target countries in our region have high entry barriers	Limited opportunities to diversify within our country	Retail banking market in our country is likely to stagnate
Reasons to enter		Reasons not to enter		Context for proposal	

Taken together, all these points may be sufficient to convince the audience that our organization ought to expand into the proposed countries, but they are not mutually exclusive. Multiple points address the same topics. Some points are subtopics of others, and some points here belong in the introduction.

In this example, the final point about the stagnation of the retail banking market in our country is the situation. The complication to that situation is in the second-to-last point: that there are limited opportunities to diversify within our country.

To create mutual exclusivity here, first move situation and complication into an introduction. Since some of the remaining points describe reasons why we should enter these countries while others describe why we should not enter all other counties, adding an additional layer of abstraction would help make the groupings mutually exclusive and more conceptually parallel.

ORGANIZE POINTS INTO MUTUALLY EXCLUSIVE GROUPS

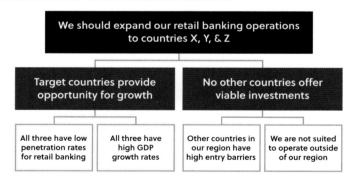

The audience no longer has to remember six interrelated points. They can remember two mutually exclusive points and use them to help remember the supporting evidence.

Collectively exhaustive

Groupings are collectively exhaustive when a group of points, taken together, addresses all aspects of the point above the group. The first step toward collective exhaustion is avoiding intellectually blank points. It is easiest to create collectively exhaustive points when the ideas the points support are well formed. This process starts with a clear situation, complication, and resolution.

As with parallelism, collectively exhaustive structures clarify the relationship between each point and the idea above it. These structures are most readily apparent when discussing part-to-whole relationships, like the divisions within a company or the components of a formula.

In the first Minto, a company splits into divisions that are collectively exhaustive. Together they account for every employee with none left out.

ONE ENTITY DIVIDED INTO PARTS

Each grouping is collectively exhaustive. Every department is either high or low impact, and every department is listed.

Calculated measures are always built out of mutually exclusive, collectively exhaustive relationships, as shown in the Minto below. Break conversations about measures of performance down into their component parts in order to create collectively exhaustive arguments about them. Consider whether your analysis can be expressed as an equation in order to help create a MECE structure for both your analysis and your communication.

ONE METRIC DIVIDED INTO INPUTS

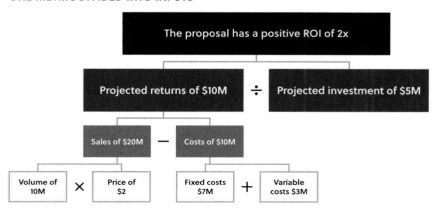

Each grouping is collectively exhaustive based on the formula for each measure. ROI is the result of returns divided by investment. Returns are the result of sales minus costs. Costs are the sum of fixed and variable costs. Sales are the product of volume and price.

In practice, audiences often forgive communications that are not fully MECE in structure. Do not confuse their charity as a signal of your logical rigor. Practice building MECE structures when the stakes are low, because rigorous structure will be most important when the problems are large, the stakes are high, and crafting MECE points is at its most challenging.

WATCH OUT: Methodology is not the output of your work

The process of generating a Minto pyramid focuses you and your audience on your findings, not the methodology that generated them. The story of why this analysis needs to exist is the story that will capture your audience. The methodology is the story of how you conducted that analysis. It should only be included to the degree that it serves the needs of the audience.

Reviewing the methodology before providing the results is the academic norm. Audiences with extensive academic training—often technical audiences—may expect and require an explanation of methodology before reviewing results.

Business audiences—who have different training—tend to focus more on results than process. They prefer to evaluate the relevance of the results before questioning the methodology. For these audiences, start with the results and explain the methodology while you are orienting the audience to the details of your analysis.

The audience will dictate when you discuss methodology and what level of detail you go into. In all cases, use a rigorous methodology to generate your results, but only review it to the degree needed to establish credibility with your audience so that you have time to discuss the results.

Support your points with sound reasoning

At some level, all data communications are persuasive communications. All seek to persuade an audience that the data presented is legitimate, the analysis is rigorous, and the findings ought to be believed. The foundation of these communications is sound logical reasoning, supported by strong, necessary, and sufficient evidence, and reinforced with a keen eye for the corrosive danger of self-deception.

Logical reasoning

All logical reasoning can be divided into one of two forms: inductive or deductive reasoning. Both can appear within a single Minto, but each group of points within a Minto can use only one approach. Most business arguments persuade with inductive reasoning.[9]

Inductive Reasoning

INDUCTIVE REASONING RESTS ON STRONG EVIDENCE

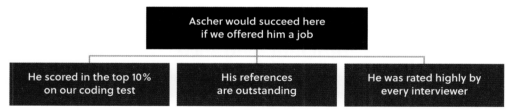

Inductive reasoning uses specific evidence to show that a broader conclusion is likely to be true. Inductively reasoned conclusions are strong when they are supported by strong evidence that is necessary and sufficient for this audience to accept the conclusion. In the example, the pyramid based on inductive reasoning uses observable evidence of Asher's job application performance to predict his success in this job.

Prior experience, analytical results, market research, commonly accepted ideas, and compelling examples can all serve as evidence depending on the situation and the audience. To convince an audience with inductive reasoning, you must provide them with the evidence they believe is necessary and sufficient to support each point. That support gets stronger as the evidence gets stronger.

---

[9] No brief explanation can do justice to the multiple millennia of thought on logical reasoning or the tremendous number of excellent resources on the topic. For those who want to dip their toe in the water, the online lessons at Khan Academy provide a structured introduction, Barbara Minto provides more business-focused examples in her book, and Wikipedia is surprisingly exhaustive on the topic.

Deductive reasoning

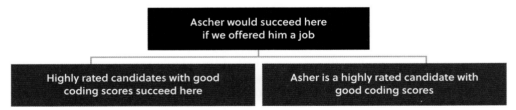

Deductive reasoning uses broad statements about what is true—called premises—rather than observable evidence to logically prove a conclusion must be true. In the deductive pyramid, the argument for Asher's success is based on the premise that highly rated candidates with good scores succeed at this role and that Asher is this type of candidate. If the audience accepts both of these statements, then they ought to accept the conclusion that Asher would succeed in this role. An expanded version of this pyramid might use inductive reasoning to support each of these premises by providing evidence for them.

Real-world systems don't generate the kinds of universally true statements on which sound deductive reasoning rests. As a result, most business reasoning is inductive—based on evidence. For that evidence to persuade, it must be necessary and sufficient to convince the audience as well as strong enough to stand up to their scrutiny.

Necessary and sufficient evidence

Ultimately, audiences decide their standard for necessary and sufficient evidence. So, you must understand the standard of evidence your audience expects in order to create an effective argument.

This standard will change based both on the scope of the argument and the individual members of the audience. The evidence that a manufacturing leadership team requires to change the safety protocol of the entire company will be more significant than the proof you need for a more narrowly scoped request to conduct a one-month trial of that protocol within a small group. Similarly, the standard of evidence required changes when the audience changes. The necessary and sufficient evidence an engineering team requires before supporting a product design change may be different from what the marketing team needs.

Identify the evidence that will be most compelling to your audience. Plan to provide every audience the full outline of your argument, but go into different levels of depth on different branches based on the audience.[10] The Minto that follows outlines an argument for a new packaging design. While every audience will likely have to believe the key ideas that the cost of rolling out the new design is low and the sales impact will be high, not

---

[10] Or, ideally, craft different communications to serve the different needs of each audience.

every audience will need the same level of detail. A marketing audience is more likely to focus on the sales impact since they will be held accountable for this outcome, while an engineering audience is more likely to press on the cost targets that they are responsible for meeting.

DIFFERENT AUDIENCES HAVE DIFFERENT STANDARDS FOR NECESSARY AND SUFFICIENT EVIDENCE

To meet engineering's standard for necessary and sufficient, you will likely need to show more evidence about cost.

To meet marketing's standard for necessary and sufficient, you will likely need to show more evidence about the sales impact.

Since the audience decides what is necessary and sufficient, you will encounter audiences where no amount of evidence will be sufficient to convince them. A manager who has had multiple bad experiences with a software platform may require unreasonable or unattainable evidence to prove that the department ought to adopt it. In these cases, consider shrinking the scope of your goal. While no amount of evidence would be sufficient to convince this manager to immediately adopt this software platform across the entire department, your evidence might be sufficient to convince them to pilot the software with a small group for six months.

Strong evidence

The stronger the evidence, the stronger your conclusion. The more often you catch your roommate taking your ice cream, cookies, and chips, the stronger the evidence becomes that your roommate is also the one stealing your candy bars. Evidence from the past, however, can never prove something about the future. A single piece of disproving evidence can always undermine your argument. Finding even a single mouse nest made of your candy bar wrappers would suggest you owe your roommate an apology.[11]

No matter how strong the evidence, you cannot force an audience to accept a conclusion, even if they believe all the evidence you have provided. It's worth remembering that only time can prove any conclusion about future events correct or incorrect. Avoid making claims of certainty regarding topics about which no one can be certain, and be wary of those that do.

Avoid self-deception

Identifying strong, necessary, and sufficient evidence is a process of choosing which data to elevate and which to discard. Conceptually, the structure of your communication is a model. Just like the model you may have built to analyze your data, it simplifies the fabulous complexity of the external world to a limited number of factors. If your analysis and your communication help the audience better understand the true nature of the challenges they face, then that simplification has the potential to help others better navigate complex choices.

Alberto Cairo, the Knight Chair of Visual Journalism at the University of Miami, named two critical strategies for designing truthful data visualizations in his book *The Truthful Art* that apply to all data-based communications:

1. Avoid self-deception.
2. Be honest with your audience.

Assuming your intention is to be honest with your audience, the remaining threat to the data is you. Or rather, it's all of us when we organize data into any sort of coherent structure, because the process itself is rife with opportunities for self-deception. Two are especially pernicious: the lure of the story and the trap of confirmation bias.[12] Outlining your thinking visually with a Minto pyramid helps mitigate the lure toward story, but any process that externalizes your thinking can bait unsophisticated users into the trap of confirmation bias.

---

[11] Logically astute readers will note that it's possible both the mouse and your roommate were stealing your candy bars. The evidence of the mouse nest is very strong evidence that the mouse took some of your candy bars, but it remains possible your roommate took some of them too. It's also possible the mouse got those candy bar wrappers from somewhere other than your pantry. Regardless, an apology to your roommate seems warranted.

[12] Cairo characterizes these as bugs in the software of the human brain. He includes a third bug: the patternicity bug. This is our tendency to see patterns everywhere, even when none exist. Chapter 3 addresses this phenomenon.

The lure of the story

Storytelling is a complex issue for those who communicate about data. While there's no universal definition of what a story is, there is widespread agreement that stories are powerful.[13] That power has the ability to move people deeply, but it also has the capacity to undermine the analytical process and the insight it can provide.

Laying out the story of the situation, complication, and resolution is a powerful way to focus your analysis on the right main idea. Storytelling in this phase of the analytical process can be powerful and effective. When conducting the analysis, however, good analysts know to be wary of explaining their analytical results through story until the analysis is complete. Since stories organize ideas into cause-and-effect chains, premature storytelling about the data can easily turn correlations into causal explanations.

Through most of human history we have explained the world primarily through stories. Imagine one awful week in a prehistorical society where a solar eclipse preceded a devastating flood. You'd be one of the reasonable ones if you believed that the sun going dark in the middle of the afternoon was the work of a very displeased supernatural being warning of impending catastrophe. Correlated events always tempt us to explain them with the clear cause and effect that stories provide. Layering emotion into stories makes these explanations even harder to dislodge.

Disciplined use of the Minto structure can help fight the temptation toward premature storytelling. Using a Minto as a framework for organizing your ideas forces you and your collaborators into the discipline of breaking down a conclusion into its component parts, testing each part, and revising your conclusion based on the findings. It can help you stay focused on conducting good science—if you can avoid the trap of confirmation bias.

The trap of confirmation bias

Confirmation bias is our tendency to disregard evidence that challenges our existing beliefs and favor evidence that supports those beliefs. Unfortunately, the process of organizing your ideas is enough to trigger the subtle effects of confirmation bias. The desire to confirm your own conclusions can alter how you analyze and present the data both consciously and unconsciously.

This effect is often magnified by organizational power structures. When the ideas you are testing come from a senior executive with more experience in the market and the industry, the pull to support their worldview is strong. When you are that senior executive, with a clear picture of your market based on years of experience, your brain can discount disconfirming evidence with terrifying ease—especially when it is spread out across different sources and time.

---

[13] The idea of a causal chain and some discussion of emotion—sometimes described as drama or tension—shows up in almost every definition of story. One of the hallmarks of human societies is their use of stories to explain the world and organize groups toward common purposes.

Any approach to analysis that forces you to express your conclusions before the analysis is complete magnifies the danger of confirmation bias. But you should avoid any temptation to abandon structure. That path is no more useful than telling scientists to abandon hypothesis-driven experimentation in favor of conducting random, unstructured experiments.

Instead, consider some of the tools scientists have been using to fight this bias. The first is conducting statistical significance tests on all your findings, even if you don't show the results to all audiences. Another is preregistration, where you share the hypothesis you are testing and your approach to testing it before conducting the analysis. This approach limits people's ability to shift their lens after the analysis is complete. While awareness of confirmation bias can help you spot it, building a process that limits its impact is far more reliably effective.

Convert your Minto pyramid into a complete communication

One of the strengths of Minto pyramids is that they support communication across a variety of channels. This section shows how a single Minto can inform a variety of communications beyond just a slide presentation, such as a written overview or a verbal update.

In the scenario that follows, the leadership of a motorbike parts manufacturer in a large developing country has asked you to investigate a new market opportunity. Currently, this manufacturer sells motorbike parts to the original equipment manufacturers of motorbikes (OEMs). The situation is that this country's economy has been growing rapidly, and the demand for new bikes has grown quickly over the last decade. The complication is that the market for new bikes is reaching saturation, but the company needs to deliver continued growth for investors. Management wants to understand the future of the OEM market and whether entering the aftermarket—the market of motorbike dealers and repair shops that purchase individual parts to service bikes—could generate more long-term growth.

In the example that follows, you have organized your research and analysis into a Minto pyramid. Leadership will use the results of your analysis to help decide if it is worthwhile to create a full market entry plan. Watch how the Minto pyramid allows you to easily convert your thinking into a slide deck, verbal update, or written summary.

ONE PYRAMID SUPPORTS A VARIETY OF COMMUNICATIONS

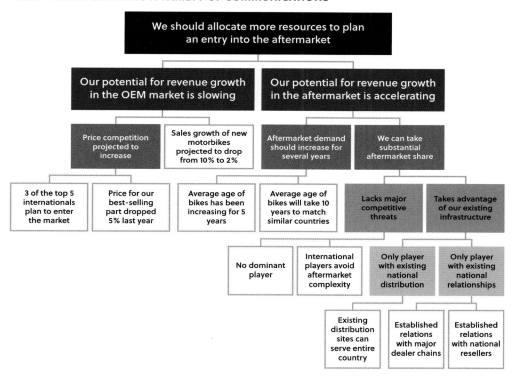

Slide presentation: Convert each evidence box into a slide

Minto pyramids readily convert into slide presentations. The main idea and key points become the agenda items that outline the presentation. Each key point becomes a section. Every evidence box converts to a slide, with the contents of each evidence box on your Minto becoming the headline of a slide. The body of each slide provides the data that supports the headline. Using this approach, you can reallocate slide creation time away from generating unnecessary slides and focus on creating powerful explanatory visualizations that pass the blink test and support your headlines.

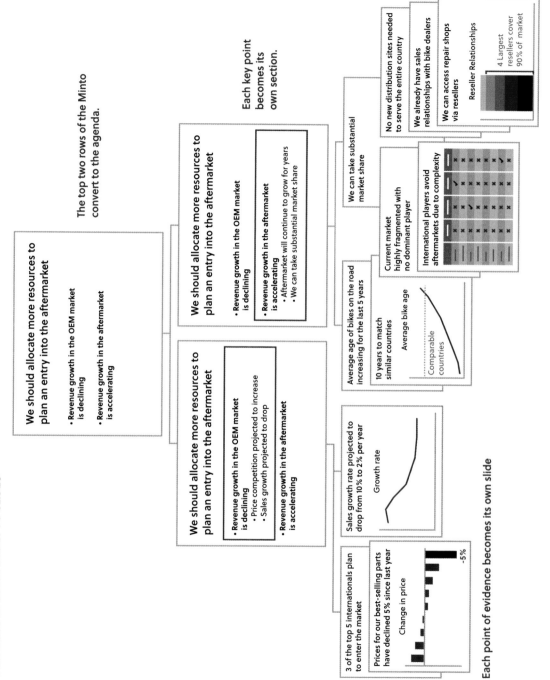

The top two rows of the Minto convert to the agenda.

Each key point becomes its own section.

We should allocate more resources to plan an entry into the aftermarket

- **Revenue growth in the OEM market is declining**
- **Revenue growth in the aftermarket is accelerating**

We should allocate more resources to plan an entry into the aftermarket

- **Revenue growth in the OEM market is declining**
- **Revenue growth in the aftermarket is accelerating**
  - Aftermarket will continue to grow for years
  - We can take substantial market share

We should allocate more resources to plan an entry into the aftermarket

- **Revenue growth in the OEM market is declining**
  - Price competition projected to increase
  - Sales growth projected to drop
- **Revenue growth in the aftermarket is accelerating**

We can take substantial market share

No new distribution sites needed to serve the entire country

We already have sales relationships with bike dealers

We can access repair shops via resellers

4 Largest resellers cover 90% of market

Reseller Relationships

Current market highly fragmented with no dominant player

International players avoid aftermarkets due to complexity

Average age of bikes on the road increasing for the last 5 years

10 years to match similar countries

Average bike age

Comparable countries

Sales growth rate projected to drop from 10% to 2% per year

Growth rate

3 of the top 5 internationals plan to enter the market

Prices for our best-selling parts have declined 5% since last year

Change in price

-5%

Each point of evidence becomes its own slide

Verbal update: Start from the main idea and work down

Below is a sample response to a question in a meeting or message thread about the findings of your research. To ease the cognitive load on the audience, always start from the top of the Minto pyramid and work down to the details. This approach avoids confusing logical leaps, provides the context your audience needs about why this matters, and allows you to adjust the level of detail to the needs of the audience in real time.

Sample verbal update based on Minto pyramid	
Provide situation and complication	"Based on your request to explore ways to maintain the company's growth rate, we've been investigating the aftermarket."
State the main idea	"Our research supports allocating more resources to create a plan to enter the aftermarket because . . ."
Share key points	"It appears that 1. Our potential for revenue growth in the OEM market is slowing. 2. Our potential for revenue growth in the aftermarket is accelerating."
Support 1st point	"We believe our growth in OEM revenue will slow over the next few years because • The growth rate of the new bike market is slowing • Price competition is increasing, driving prices down."
Support 2nd point	"We believe our potential for growth in the aftermarket is accelerating because • The market will continue to grow over the next ten years. • We have the potential to capture substantial market share."
Review key points	"So, based on the 1. Decreased potential for growth in the OEM market 2. Increased potential for growth in the aftermarket . . ."
Review main idea	"We should allocate more resources to create a plan to enter the aftermarket."

For a senior-level audience, this update might suffice. If you have organized your ideas well, you can confidently go deeper on any questions the audience has. Use the same approach of working down one branch of your pyramid, starting from whatever point best addresses the question. Preview the next level of points, go through each one explaining the evidence that supports them, and end by recapping the same points.

Audiences with specialized knowledge may want to jump to points even further down on larger Minto pyramids. If one person wants to jump directly to a deeper-level issue, make sure to verbally work down your Minto pyramid without skipping over any logic so that everyone in the audience will understand how that point logically connects to the main idea.[14]

Written summary: Each group becomes a section

Minto pyramids can generate clear written updates. Just as in conversation or slides, allow the organization of your pyramid to drive the structure of your written document. Preview your main idea and key points in the introduction. Unpack each key idea within its own section, and support each idea with evidence.

---

[14] This general advice has many exceptions to it. Use your knowledge of the audience as a guide. Specific technical questions with clear answers may be dispensed with via a quick, direct answer if you are confident that answer will satisfy the audience member and not introduce additional questions from other audience members. Aim to balance the needs of individual audience members with the needs of the audience as a whole, without losing focus on the needs of the key decision-makers.

Main idea

Introduction previews the key points

Subject: Aftermarket is growing and worth investigating further

In order to maintain the company's growth, we recommend a deeper investigation into the costs and returns of entering the aftermarket because:

- Our potential for revenue growth in the OEM market is slowing.
- Our potential for revenue growth in the aftermarket is accelerating.

Each key point becomes a section

Revenue growth in the OEM market is slowing

We believe the market for selling parts to the original equipment manufacturers of motorbikes will become less attractive in the future. Over the history of the company, this market has shown consistently high growth and supported premium prices. *Our projections suggest that even though the market will continue to grow, it will do so at a much slower rate, and increased competition will drive down prices for our products.*

Lowest level evidence in Minto becomes supporting evidence

Market growth, which has been over 10% per year for the last decade, will slow to 2% over the next five years. The past growth has been driven by an increasing share of the population purchasing motorbikes. As we approach market saturation, the growth of the motorbike market will slow. Within five years, the primary driver of new motorbike sales will be population growth.

As market growth slows, *we expect price competition to increase.* The average selling price for our top-selling part already declined 5% last year due to competition. Three of the top five international players have announced plans to enter our market. These players enjoy major economies of scale, allowing them to undercut us on price. Prices have declined 10–20% in other markets they have entered, and we expect a similar impact on our business.

Section intro previews the next level of points

Revenue growth potential in the aftermarket is accelerating

Our research suggests the aftermarket will become a more attractive market for us in the future as maintenance needs increase. We think we are uniquely positioned to capture aftermarket share because the domestic aftermarket currently lacks a dominant player, and our existing distribution network provides a unique competitive advantage.

Each sub-point becomes a paragraph

The need for replacement parts will grow as the average age of bikes on the road increases. Over the past five years, the average age of bikes on the road has already doubled from one and a half years old to three years old. In ten years, the average bike will be five years old. This change will drive a substantial increase in demand for replacement parts, as the average motorbike needs key parts replaced starting at year four.

The fragmented aftermarket has room for a large player to pick up significant market share. Currently no player controls more than 5% of the aftermarket, allowing space for a major player to pick up large segments of the market. International players are unlikely to compete here. They have avoided the complexities of the aftermarket in other countries they have entered.

Our existing national distribution system provides us a unique advantage in this space. We can support one-day shipping to 83% of the dealers and repair shops that purchase aftermarket parts without building additional distribution sites. From a sales point of view, we already have relationships with dealers (who often service bikes) via our OEM relationships, and we can reach 90% of the remaining market using only four resellers.

Conclusion reinforces key points and restates main idea

Aftermarket warrants deeper investigation

As the OEM market moves toward lower growth and prices, the growth in the aftermarket offers a chance to leverage our unique national distribution network. Based on this initial investigation, we recommend allocating the resources required to create a detailed market entry plan for the aftermarket.

Key concepts from this chapter

Sound structure is the foundation on which effective communication is built.

THE MINTO PYRAMID CHECKLIST

Does your Minto	Test your Minto pyramid
Have a clear structure?	• Does every point in a group answer the same question implied by the box above it? • Does every point summarize all the boxes below it? • Does every branch of your tree end at evidence?
Take advantage of story to identify the main idea?	• Do you understand which ideas the audience already accepts that describe the situation? • Have you identified a complication that introduces a problem this audience will believe needs to be solved? • Does your main idea resolve the tension between the situation and the complication?
Support your main idea with the right key points?	• Have you tried to build your pyramid from the top down? • Have you sought feedback from others? • Have you avoided intellectually blank ideas? • Have you confronted nonsupporting evidence?
Organize the points to minimize cognitive load?	• Is every grouping grammatically and conceptually parallel? • Is every grouping ordered meaningfully? • Is every grouping mutually exclusive and collectively exhaustive (MECE)?
Rest on a foundation of strong logical reasoning?	• Have you provided necessary and sufficient evidence for this audience to accept your conclusions? • Have you provided strong evidence that will hold up on inspection by your audience? • Have you taken steps to limit self-deception?

If you remember nothing else . . .

Clarify the story that generated this analysis to get to the right main idea.

Default to the top-down approach whenever possible and start building your outline from a main idea.

The needs of the audience determine what evidence is necessary and sufficient to convince them.

Focus on the analysis that will persuade, not the data that is easiest to collect.

Be careful of explaining the results with a story until the analysis is complete.

Exercise: Making the case at Craigstone—Part I

Using the case facts below, select a preferred travel provider. Identify the situation, the complication, and resolution. Then, craft a Minto pyramid outlining the argument in favor of that travel provider.

Case background

Craigstone is a fast-growing management consulting firm that employs roughly 250 people with offices in North America, Europe, and Latin America. The company's headquarters is in Boston, Massachusetts. The company experienced consistent growth over its first three decades. The first year of declining revenue in over a decade was in in 2020, due to the economic impact of COVID-19. Craigstone emerged from the crisis with its core business intact, but it is now more focused on controlling costs than ever before.

Even though Craigstone's travel expenses are 60% lower per person than they were before COVID-19, client complaints about travel costs have doubled. Clients pay Craigstone employees' travel costs in addition to the fees they pay the firm. Craigstone has always allowed employees to book airline flights, hotels, and rental cars on their personal credit cards through whatever website or travel agent they choose. The firm's largest client, which is also its only Fortune 100 client, has threatened to end its growing relationship with the firm as travel costs have started to exceed 15% of their consulting fees. The company's growth plan requires the firm to add other very large clients to its client roster. Though travel costs have traditionally been passed on to clients, competitive firms are increasingly absorbing travel costs in their fees and attempting to reduce the cost to clients without lowering prices.

To address travel costs, the firm has created a committee of five partners and an analyst to analyze the firm's travel policies. The goal is to recommend ways to reduce costs and streamline policies that have until now been handled in an ad hoc manner.

CRAIGSTONE FACTS

	2017	2018	2019	2020	2021
Revenue	$81.7M	$105M	$121M	$90.8M	$99.5M
Travel costs	$8.7M	$11.5M	$13.8M	$2.5M	$6.0M
Head count	212	262	290	259	250
Offices	7	9	9	8	8

The committee's findings

After some initial discussions within the committee's membership and with others across the company, the analyst compiled the data and presented it to the partners on the committee. The data suggests that consolidating travel spending through a single partner could allow Craigstone to realize substantial savings. After talking to several large travel vendors, the committee has come to a consensus that the choice is between two serious contenders: LanaTravel.com and Canadian Express. Both offer savings on travel for firms that book at least $5M worth of business through them. With both services, consultants would continue to select their own itineraries and have access to all major airlines, hotels, and transportation services.

In comparing the travel agencies, the analysts compiled the following facts

1. **LanaTravel.com:** Lana is a four-year-old fast-growing start-up that combines a travel booking app for users with a reporting app for Craigstone's finance team. The app is exceptionally well-designed, and even though the company is not profitable, it has been funded by prominent venture capital firms.[15] The younger employees at Craigstone have expressed strong enthusiasm for the app's usability, since they prefer to book and manage travel via a phone app. Many like that the app also allows them to manage all their travel reward programs in one place. Lana offers live phone support during East Coast business hours but only guarantees 24/7 support via the chat function in their app. Consultants frequently change travel plans and have complex itineraries. More senior members of the firm say that they need to be able to call a live human any time of the day or night. This is a major concern for them. Lana negotiates discounted rates with airlines, hotels, and other large travel providers. They say the average company saves 6% on travel costs by using them, and they guarantee at least a 4% savings. User reviews report that the app is slow and glitchy in China, which is a major growth area for the business, but many firms similar in size to Craigstone have adopted the service and report that they are satisfied with it. Some Craigstone partners have expressed concern that Lana may not be around long term. They don't want to go through this process again.

2. **Canadian Express:** CanEx, as it is known, is a major financial services company with a global credit card business in addition to its travel business. It is a large and stable company that has been in business for over 170 years. They are the industry standard for the world's largest consulting firms. They have a full-featured website for booking and changing travel (though it is not as robust and easy to use as Lana) and excellent live support. Agents are available by phone 24/7 from anywhere in the world. The company guarantees a 5% discount on

---

[15] Venture capital is a class of investment that funds early-stage, high-risk businesses. While most companies backed by venture capital fail, many consider the prominence of the venture capital firm a predictor of the company's likelihood of success.

travel booked through them and has another, related feature that could save Craigstone even more. Craigstone could gain an additional 1% reduction on all travel expenses charged through CanEx credit cards. Finance says that moving the company to CanEx cards would automate travel reimbursements. These currently take over a month, which is a substantial burden on many employees. CanEx says its credit card perks are competitive with the best reward cards on the market, but switching between credit cards to take advantage of different rewards from different companies is a hobby for a meaningful number of consultants. They consider it an important employment perk.

Case adapted from a case originally developed by JoAnne Yates and the Management Communications Group at the MIT Sloan School of Management.

Frame the Data to Persuade

(so the audience acts)

———

Source: https://xkcd.com/106

This chapter introduces the factors that influence your audience beyond the quality of your analysis and the clarity of your structure. It discusses how the audience's prior knowledge and biases should influence your approach. The Elaboration Likelihood Model provides a framework for understanding how nondata factors inform the audience's decision-making process, and the remainder of the chapter presents strategies to maximize the impact of your communication by explaining What's In It For Them—the WIIFT—and framing your points around common thinking patterns. The exercise challenges you to create Minto pyramids designed for specific audiences.

Audiences evaluate more than just the data

Strong evidence and clear structure form the foundation of effective data communications. Yet sometimes even rock-solid analysis and airtight reasoning fail to persuade others. Even worse, weak evidence and muddled logic often still move others to action. The frustrating reality is that audiences are people, and people are complicated.

The science explaining how people evaluate information is equally complicated. It suggests both that we have a strong desire to explain the world through narrative and that our intuition often fails us when we interpret the implications of quantitative information. Many of our failures to evaluate data accurately are the result of systematic, reproducible errors in thinking called cognitive biases.[1] Fortunately, the consistency of these biases allows us to adopt strategies that mitigate them.

The Elaboration Likelihood Model—presented in this chapter—helps explain whether the content of the analysis or its delivery will more heavily influence your audience. Based on that understanding, you can develop clearer explanations of What's In It For Them—the WIIFT—to maximize the audience's engagement with your content, better establish your credibility, and reframe your points to increase their impact.

Understand how audiences evaluate your ideas

The more personally relevant an outcome is to your audience, the more deeply your audience will engage with the content and evidence that supports it. The less clearly relevant the issue is, the more heavily your audience will focus on factors related to their relationship with the communicator and how the message is delivered. You can imagine these two different responses to your communication as the extremes of a continuum.

On one end of the spectrum is something persuasion theorists call central processing. When central processing is used, audiences focus more on the message itself, the quality of the argument, and the data that supports it. People engaging central processing are more willing to tolerate high cognitive load in their decision-making.

---

[1] A deep dive into cognitive biases is a worthwhile exploration for anyone who makes decisions. Daniel Kahneman's *Thinking, Fast and Slow* is a great starting point, as are *Nudge* by Richard Thaler and Cass Sunstein and *Predictably Irrational* by Daniel Ariely.

As a result, they are likely to factor the content of the message more heavily into their decision-making.

On the other end of the continuum is peripheral processing. When people use peripheral processing, they rely more on factors related to how the message is delivered, who is communicating it, and how well the message conforms to a variety of mental shortcuts humans use to make quick decisions.

The same person will use different routes for different decisions, or even for the same decision at different times. Many factors influence the route used, but the higher the stakes and the more personally relevant the implications are, the more likely someone is to take the central processing route.

THE ELABORATION LIKELIHOOD MODEL OF AUDIENCE PROCESSING ROUTES

Central processing	Peripheral processing
Audiences expend more cognitive energy *"The path of high elaboration"*	Audiences expend less cognitive energy *"The path of low elaboration"*
Tends to be used when The audience believes the topic is personally relevant and has the ability to mentally focus	**Tends to be used when** The audience does not believe the topic is personally relevant and/or does not have the ability to mentally focus
Audience focus The content and evidence of the message	**Audience focus** The framing and delivery of the message and their relationship to the communicator

A subtle but important distinction is that the processing route is not defined by the external factors an individual uses to evaluate the argument. It is defined by the individual's internal thought process. Central processing involves effortful, deliberate consideration. Peripheral processing involves more automatic responses. Factors traditionally associated with peripheral processing can be used in central processing if they are explicitly considered. For example, knowledge that a high-ranking, influential leader has accepted the results of an analysis might exert an unconscious, automatic influence on the audience's decision-making. That is peripheral processing. An audience using central processing might use the same knowledge as an input to their decision-making, but they would do so explicitly. They might carefully consider the strategic impact of aligning themselves with or against this influential leader. The factor is the same, but it's thought about differently.

This model of thinking is called the Elaboration Likelihood Model (ELM),[2] named for the idea that in central processing individuals are more willing to elaborate on the content of an argument. The ELM is useful for data communicators because it reminds you that audiences incorporate factors beyond the data itself when they evaluate your conclusions.

Communicators try to engage central processing

Audiences are most likely to take the central processing route when they believe a topic is high stakes and personally relevant. This is what the ELM calls the path of high elaboration, where individuals expend significant cognitive energy on a topic. Members of the audience using this route will be more likely to factor the quality of your evidence and depth of your reasoning into their decision to accept or reject your conclusions. Though communicators tend to prefer the deeper consideration central processing brings with it, engaging central processing doesn't make you more persuasive. It does make the audience more likely to form their response based on your content and to hold tighter to whatever conclusion they reach, even when faced with future counterarguments.[3]

Since personal relevance best predicts which route an audience takes, explaining the impact your findings will have on the audience—What's In It For Them—is the single most powerful tool you have to engage their central processing.

Another predictor of the audience's likelihood to engage their central processing is the audience's ability to engage with the content. Interruptions during a communication—like text messages or background noise—make it more difficult for audiences to engage central processing. Combat these distractions with a clear argument, structured to minimize cognitive load. Try to get people's full, in-person attention for critical issues that require central processing.

---

[2] There are a variety of models that attempt to describe decision-making in general and persuasion in particular. Like any model that's been around for forty years, there are multiple reasonable challenges to the ELM. Like every model, it's a simplification of reality that is intended to increase clarity.

[3] This book focuses on day-to-day business decision-making where we assume that strong evidence has the power to change opinions. Researchers have found that decision-making behaves differently when it touches on issues that people use to define their worldview, as is the case for many political topics. Opinions about sales commission plans may be strongly held, but they don't tend to define how we see the world. Strong evidence that a different commission plan would work better does tend to change minds, albeit more slowly than the persuader might like. Opinions about what constitutes a fair criminal justice system, on the other hand, tend to be much more intertwined with the group affiliations by which we define ourselves. Research suggests people respond differently to evidence challenging these kinds of identity-defining opinions. When presented with evidence that contradicts positions people use to define their identities, people tend to harden their preexisting beliefs and become more resistant to persuasion. The stronger the evidence against their position, the more it tends to harden their existing opinion. This is, without a doubt, the most disheartening note in this book. Better understanding the phenomenon and how to correct for it is one of the most important social and political considerations of our time. See D. Flynn, B. Nyhan, and J. Reifler, "The Nature and Origins of Misperceptions: Understanding False and Unsupported Beliefs About Politics," *Advances in Political Psychology*, 38 (2017): 127–150.

Audiences use peripheral processing most of the time

Central processing is cognitively expensive. Audiences can afford to engage it only on a limited number of topics. Assume audiences want to avoid the cognitive burden associated with this route and tend toward peripheral processing unless the stakes and personal relevance of your topic are clear.

Peripheral processing is the path of low elaboration. Audiences using this path tend to rely on signals that are easier to evaluate than the data and argument itself, such as the credibility of the speaker. Compared to the central processing route, this route relies less on the quality of the reasoning than on how the content is framed and delivered.

Audiences using the peripheral route can be frustrating or satisfying depending on their biases. They engage less with the data. Nondata factors sway them more easily. This can result in situations ranging from easy agreement with your conclusions to fierce resistance that even the strongest evidence cannot overcome. Regardless, the opinions people form with peripheral processing are more likely to evaporate in the face of future challenges than those formed with central processing.

Despite your best efforts, expect most audiences to use peripheral processing most of the time. There is simply too much information, and too many decisions to be made, to process everything using the central processing route. Effective communicators accept that audiences use a variety of factors to evaluate information. They create communications that appeal to both processing channels, and increase their likelihood of engaging central processing by establishing What's In It For Them for every audience.

Maximize the likelihood of central processing with the WIIFT

The most effective way to engage your audience's central processing route is to explain What's In It For Them—the WIIFT[4]—within the main idea of every communication. A WIIFT statement describes how this communication is relevant to individual audience members by explaining how they benefit from understanding the data or taking the action proposed.

Too few communicators take the time to articulate the WIIFT. As a result, audiences fail to see the relevance of many communications and disengage. If the information you are communicating has no implications for the audience, you will not be able to craft a WIIFT statement. More often, however, some aspect of your communication impacts the audience's lives, no matter how abstractly. If this audience benefits from understanding what you have to say, there is a WIIFT.

Craft strong WIIFTs by
- Connecting your main idea to its concrete impact on the audience's lives
- Explaining why this idea matters to them
- Changing the WIIFT when the audience changes

Connect your main idea to its impact on audience members' lives

To explain the WIIFT, you must understand what matters to the individual members of your audience and how this information impacts them personally. Consider all the factors that impact your audience's day-to-day experiences. Use answers to questions like these to help generate strong WIIFTs.

- What impact might this topic have on the ease or difficulty of their day-to-day work?
- What impact might this data have on how they are evaluated and compensated?
- What impact might these findings have on their ability to secure the resources and people they need to accomplish their goals?
- What impact might this proposal have on the audience's status within the organization?

---

[4] The concept of explaining how ideas benefit the audience is much more widespread than this specific acronym. Should you want to popularize it within your workplace, it's typically pronounced "whiff-tee."

Since strong WIIFTs speak to individuals, the WIIFT changes when the audience changes. Remember that organizations are made up of people whose goals may or not may not be aligned with those of the organization. Groups and individuals may actively oppose changes that shift resources away from them. WIIFTs work because they address this reality. They force you to ask yourself the question your audience is always trying to answer: what does this mean for me?

In the sample scenarios below note how the WIIFT addresses some impact each topic has on the audience.

Audience	Topic	Why does this topic matter to this audience?	Sample WIIFT
CFO	Cash projections	The CFO is responsible for making sure the company has enough cash on hand.	We need a 20% credit line increase by the end of this quarter to be able to pay employees.
Marketing director	Marketing allocation	Individual performance is measured by ROI.	Reallocating marketing spending to online programs could double marketing ROI.
IT managers	Data security	The company disciplines people who violate the company's privacy policy.	Understand the company's data security protocols to avoid disciplinary action.
All non-managers	Employee satisfaction survey	Managers are a primary driver of workplace satisfaction.	Fill out the employee satisfaction survey so we can allocate bonuses to the best managers.

Ask yourself why this idea matters to them

The examples that follow show the thought processes different authors went through to get from a generic main idea to a WIIFT statement. They asked themselves why this topic matters to this audience and what impact this information will have on the audience. Using the answers to these questions, the authors revised their main idea into a WIIFT statement.

Example 1: Articulate the problem clearly

Original main idea	Revenue analysis suggests there are issues in our claims process.
Intended audience	Billing team within a large medical practice
Author	A physician and co-owner of a large medical practice investigating the practice's decline in revenue over the past year
Why does this matter to this audience?	Insurance companies have been denying an increasing number of claims for reimbursement. The decrease in claim approvals explains almost all of the revenue decline over the last year. A continued decline in revenue could lead to job losses.
What impact does this have on this audience?	The insurance company is denying most claims because of insufficient or incorrect information. The billing team is responsible for verifying that claims are submitted with sufficient, correct information.
Revised WIIFT	Revenue analysis shows that reducing the number of claims denied due to insufficient information by 20% would turn our 5% revenue decline into a 10% revenue increase.

Clarifying the main idea helped clarify the WIIFT

Peers felt that the author's original main idea was vague. Both the potential causes and effects were unclear. The author recognized this but feared that explaining the problem as a billing problem would put the billing team on the defensive. The author didn't want to alienate the team most needed to solve this problem.

Peers pointed out that the billing team had the power to turn around the firm's revenue decline. They asked why the billing team wasn't already working on this. The author realized that the billing team probably did not realize the impact denied claims were having on the practice's revenue. Based on this thinking, the author set out to create a WIIFT that helped the billing team understand how a change in their actions could impact the entire practice.

In order to do so, the author quantified the impact of a reasonably sized change in claim denials on overall revenue. The author felt a 20% increase in claim acceptance was an achievable target. It avoided the suggestion that the billing team needed to achieve 100% claim acceptance rates—an impossible standard.

Showing them the impact of reducing claim denials helped the billing team recognize the problem and motivated them to identify solutions. They helped build new processes for the entire staff that enabled everyone to generate more complete claims.

Example 2: Clarify the scope and time frame

Original main idea	We must prioritize analyzing why customers using dual-factor authentication have such low transaction success rates.[5]
Intended audience	Engineering leadership team at a large bank
Author	Lead engineer on the website development team at a large bank
Why does this matter to this audience?	Currently customers can use either single-factor or dual-factor authentication for large transactions on the bank's website. The engineering team committed to requiring dual-factor authentication for all large transactions by the end of next quarter. This commitment was a highly visible output of the team's yearly goal setting process, and it had been presented to the board of directors. Currently, transactions with dual-factor authentication fail four times more often than those using the secure single-factor method.
What impact does this have on this audience?	If the team cannot identify why the current process fails so often, it cannot engineer an effective solution. Without a solution, the team will be forced to either miss the deadline or require customers to adopt the current dual-factor authentication experience. The high failure rate of the current dual-factor authentication experience will generate a large number of customer complaints. Both would be highly visible failures for the team.
Revised WIIFT	We will not be able to meet the commitment we made to implement dual-factor authentication by the end of Q3 unless we understand why dual-factor authentication continues to fail for 40% of transactions, compared with our 10% failure rate for single-factor authentication.

Reminding the audience of the time frame and magnitude helped create urgency

Peers pushed the author to demonstrate the personal relevance of the problem by explaining why it was so urgent. The author had assumed the audience understood the urgency of this request because the author brought the issue up in every meeting. Reflecting on the problem, the author realized that the discussion usually devolved into an argument about the potential causes of the problem, rather than a discussion about the deadline or the importance of the commitment. The author's revised WIIFT reminded the audience of the project's visibility and quantified the scale of the problem.

---

[5] Dual-factor authentication is an online security protocol where users have to present two pieces of evidence confirming they are who they say they are. Submitting both your password and a unique code texted to your phone is an example of dual-factor authentication. In this example, a successful transaction is any time a user enters both factors correctly. If either factor is incorrect, it is considered a failed transaction. A user who mistyped their password four times and then typed it correctly on the fifth attempt would have generated four failed transactions and one successful transaction—a 20% success rate.

None of this was new information to the team, but they had never thought about the magnitude of the problem, the urgency of the deadline, and the visibility of the project at the same time. Since the author had been assigned to champion this initiative, the audience assumed that the author would remind them of anything they needed to remember. When they heard all the issues synthesized into a single main idea, the team recognized the importance of the project and reallocated several engineers' time to conduct a more thorough investigation.

Example 3: Connect the proposal to a shared goal

Original main idea	We should adopt the content management system (CMS)[6] used by one of our subdivisions across the entire division.
Intended audience	Division leadership team
Author	The manager responsible for deploying and maintaining this CMS with a subdivision of a large publishing conglomerate
Why does this matter to this audience?	The company's CEO issued a high-profile mandate to save costs and increase efficiency by consolidating the organization onto a smaller number of technology platforms. Division leadership's compensation is tied to these goals. Currently, multiple overlapping technologies are used throughout the company, even within individual divisions.
What impact does this have on this audience?	Implementation will require meaningful time from everyone in the audience. Adopting this proposal means there will be less time for other proposals. A successful adoption within this division could set up this technology for adoption across the company, which would save this division time in the long term and set up members of its leadership team for larger roles within the organization.
Revised WIIFT	We should adopt the CMS platform developed by our subdivision because it is our best-developed and best-managed CMS. Adopting it will be the most efficient way to meet the CEO's mandate to save costs and increase efficiency with a shared technology.

---

[6] Content management systems are used to manage digital content like text, photos, and videos. They generally allow multiple people to access and edit content, control permissions on who can modify which content, and support the processes of creating, reviewing, and publishing content, especially for online or offline publication.

**Connecting the proposal to a shared goal helped explain why
this audience should care**

Peers felt the author made a strong proposal, but they weren't clear about the benefits or the stakes. The author realized that the primary benefit of this proposal was that it offered a chance to address the CEO's mandate in the least disruptive way possible. Making progress on this goal could improve both the audience's compensation and their long-term futures within the organization, but failing would have an even more visible negative impact.

Focusing on the CEO's mandate to consolidate technologies framed this proposal around a goal that the entire leadership team cared about and one that was tied to personal benefits.[7] The author focused on efficiency in order to emphasize that this was a lower-risk proposal than the other options under consideration. The lower risk and alignment with the CEO's goal separated this proposal from other initiatives designed to increase productivity or drive revenue. By connecting this proposal to a goal shared by the entire leadership team, the author was able to engage the team in serious consideration of the proposal.

Change the WIIFT when the audience changes

Since the WIIFT explains why this topic matters to this audience, different audiences require different WIIFTs, even on the same topic. Plan to craft a new WIIFT for every audience, even if it's the only thing you change about your communication. The example below takes one topic and compares the WIIFT for three different audiences. Each WIIFT emerges from the issues and the impact this proposal has on each audience.

The author is the head of accounts payable (AP) at a fast-growing manufacturer of high-end dental equipment. AP is responsible for paying all the company's vendors and suppliers. The company prides itself on being the first to market with new, state-of-the-art dental technology. They encourage employees to purchase any tools or equipment that would help them do their jobs more efficiently.

When the company was smaller, managers would send an email to AP to approve employee purchases. Now that the company is bigger, the volume of purchases is too large to handle over email. AP has implemented a new online purchase approval system and needs to train employees to use it. The system is not complicated, but it is different.

Employees get notifications about new systems almost every week and often ignore them. The author worried that another email about a new system would be easy to dismiss. The more people who continue to use the older system, the more time it will take the AP staff to retrain them and the more they are likely to complain. As a support function, AP is judged in large part on the satisfaction reported by others in the organization.

---

[7] It is important to note here that compensation was tied to this goal. This is an appeal to their self-interest, not just an appeal to follow a corporate mandate. Appeals to corporate visions or goals that do not directly benefit the audience often result in nods of agreement when others are watching, followed by inaction.

For the purposes of this issue, the author divided the company into three main audiences: senior leaders who are responsible for the overall health and success of the company, managers who have to approve the purchases that employees make, and the employees who make those purchases. While managers make some larger purchases that senior leadership must approve, these purchases are rare and so large that they are often treated as special cases.

Audience 1: Senior leadership

Senior Leadership WIIFT	The new purchasing process will streamline purchase approvals and allow us to generate more accurate spending forecasts faster. Beyond that benefit, it should not have a significant effect on your workflow.

Why does this matter to senior leadership?
The new purchase approval system will allow AP to give senior leadership faster and more accurate reports on the company's spending. Senior leadership can use this information to make decisions about where to invest resources. Managing cash is important to the company's core operations. The company has to spend money to build its products long before it gets paid for them. The more cash available, the more product the company can manufacture and the more easily it can satisfy customer demand. Better cash forecasting reduces the risk involved in those decisions.

What impact does this have on senior leadership?
The new system will have virtually no impact on their day-to-day lives. They shouldn't even notice a change unless managers complain.

Main idea and WIIFT for senior leadership
The author identified that most of the benefits to senior leadership from this system come in the form of improved reporting. Senior leaders have to process a lot of incoming information, and the author felt that relieving them of the need to understand this new system would build credibility for future requests that require their attention. The author focused the WIIFT for this audience on the benefit of not having to do anything or understand much about the new system.

Audience 2: Managers

Manager WIIFT	Understanding the new purchase approval process will save you time by allowing you to approve and track all your purchase requests in one place and help AP resolve approval delays faster.

Why does this matter to managers?
Managers in this organization approve employee purchase requests. Delayed approvals slow employees down and reduce their productivity. They also generate complaints from employees that result in manager complaints to accounts payable. If the new system works well, it should reduce the amount of time managers have to spend following up on requests currently getting lost in an email-based system and reduce complaints.

What impact does this have on managers?
This changes managers' workflow substantially. If adopted properly, the author believes it will save them time. If they or their team members do not adopt the new process, it will delay purchase approvals and require managers to spend time chasing employees to resubmit their requests.

Main idea and WIIFT for managers
The author chose to focus the manager WIIFT on the time savings. This WIIFT explains how this system saves managers time by centralizing purchase requests and reducing approval delays. The author hoped this benefit would encourage managers to find out more about the new system, so they can capture those time savings. For managers who don't find the current process burdensome, the author acknowledged that this WIIFT would have limited appeal, but noted that these managers also tend to have the fewest purchase requests.

Audience 3: Employees

Employee WIIFT	To receive approval for purchases, you will need to submit requests through our new system. Understanding and using the new system will help you receive your purchases faster.

Why does this matter to employees?
Employees purchase equipment and tools to facilitate their work. The easier and faster it is to get purchases approved, the more easily they can do their jobs.

What impact does this have on employees?

This changes the process for approving purchases. It's more standardized than the prior system but less flexible. Previously, employees just had to send an email to their manager. This new system will probably slow them down at first. It will reduce approval delays, but no individual employee tends to experience many approval delays. So, the benefit of faster approvals won't be very powerful for this audience.

Main idea and WIIFT for employees

The author noted that this change requires employees to learn a new system and doesn't generate significant benefits for any single individual. This change moves the company from a flexible system to a less flexible one, and it introduces a new process that most employees only need to use a few times a year.

As a result, the author struggled to identify a powerful benefit to this audience, which was even more frustrating because this audience has to bear most of the switching costs. The primary benefit the author found was that the new system would be the only way for employees to get purchases approved. The author focused on this impact and avoided using benefits that primarily accrue to others—like improved reporting and centralization—to convince this audience. The author focused on the speed of receiving purchases, not the speed of approvals, because the arrival of a purchase represents a more concrete impact on the employee's experience.

> **WATCH OUT: Establish the WIIFT, even when it's "just informational"**
>
> Communications that are not intended to persuade the audience do not excuse the communicator from establishing What's In It For Them. Unlike persuasive communications, informational presentations are easier to dismiss, delete, or disengage from because they do not ask the audience to explicitly accept or do anything.
>
> As a result, it is more important to explain why informational communications matter to an audience and what impact this information has on their lives. Use the WIIFT to explain to the audience how this data impacts them and why engaging with it is a valuable use of their time.

Take advantage of peripheral processing signals

Audiences try to conserve cognitive effort. While well-structured communications with clear WIIFTs told as stories can reduce the burden of central processing, at least some peripheral processing tends to influence all thinking. Effective communicators appeal to all the factors an audience uses to evaluate their analysis.

One cognitive bias that helps explain the importance of a multipronged approach is substitution.[8] The substitution bias is our tendency to automatically substitute complex, hard-to-evaluate problems with ones that are less mentally taxing. We do this without conscious thought. For example, when faced with the cognitively demanding challenge of evaluating the credibility of your analysis, audiences often substitute a question that is much easier to evaluate emotionally: does the communicator of this analysis seem credible?

Effective communicators recognize the power of biases like substitution and look for ways to use them to lower cognitive load on the audience without distorting the data. They instead look for signals that audiences respond to and amplify them. In particular, they consider how to emphasize believable sources of their credibility and how to frame their points in line with common thinking patterns.

Emphasize sources of credibility

Since your audience can evaluate how credible you seem much more easily than they can evaluate the credibility of your analysis, make sure you have thought through the signals of credibility you want to emphasize. While you cannot manufacture credibility, you can amplify the signals of credibility that are most likely to resonate. Rank, expertise, goodwill, and common ground with the audience all represent sources of credibility.[9]

Rank

Rank is your formal position within the organization. If your organization is hierarchical, a high rank may be an important source of credibility. If you are of higher rank than the audience, emphasize it as appropriate. If your rank is lower than the audience, consider borrowing the credibility of someone whose rank is higher. Approaches for doing this range from mentioning the approval of a more senior person to having someone of higher rank deliver the message. If rank is not a major source of credibility within your organization, avoid emphasizing it.

---

[8] Substitution bias is also called attribute substitution.

[9] The factors discussed in this chapter are adapted from those listed in Mary Munter and Lynn Hamilton's *Guide to Managerial Communications*, now sadly out of print, based on the work of social power theorists French, Raven, and Kotter.

Expertise

Expertise is the audience's perception of your knowledge on this topic. Remember, their perception may or may not align with reality. When the audience is unaware of your expertise, consider sharing how you gained it. Focus on verifiable facts like time spent working on certain types of problems and concrete outcomes. When your perceived expertise is low, align yourself with recognized experts on the topic by incorporating sources the audience finds credible.

Above all else, demonstrate your expertise with the clarity of your communication rather than the level of detail you go into. Trust that the evidence of your hard work and competence will emerge from the clarity of your thinking, not the amount of data you cram onto a slide.

Goodwill

Goodwill is the positive feeling an audience holds toward you. Your goodwill is based on both your prior interactions with the audience and your reputation.

The prior interaction aspect of goodwill can be thought of like a bank account. Lean on the bank account aspect of goodwill by making deposits before they are needed.[10] Support others when you don't have to. Seek out opportunities to better their lives in small and large ways, especially when the cost to you is low. Emphasize your goodwill by tactfully reminding the audience of your prior positive interactions.

The reputation aspect of goodwill functions less like a bank account and more like a tree. A strong reputation grows slowly, fed by sustained, consistent evidence of trustworthiness and performance. However, it can be toppled by a single act that shows you are untrustworthy. Build your reputation by being honest and clear. In your communications, be explicit about how your conclusions impact the audience with an honest WIIFT. Provide a balanced assessment of the facts, and disclose conflicts of interest. Prepare well so that you can answer relevant questions, and defer less relevant questions without undermining your credibility.

Common ground

Common ground is the audience's belief that you share their values and goals. Emphasize common ground by being explicit about shared values and goals. Talk about the ways in which you are similar to the audience.[11] Aim to frame the WIIFT around benefits that accrue to both you and the audience to increase common ground.

---

[10] Students of persuasion will recognize this as Robert Cialdini's Principle of Reciprocity. This chapter focuses on principles of persuasion that have particular relevance to data. Understanding the principles of persuasion is a critical skill for all communicators, and Cialdini's book—*Influence: The Psychology of Persuasion*—remains an excellent place to start.

[11] As with all the qualities in this section, good judgment and tact are essential. The audience determines similarity, so understand what counts for them. A friend once heard a speaker tell an audience of military veterans transitioning from active service to graduate business school that she knew *exactly* what they were going through because her son was a veteran. The audience did not find this to be a credible similarity. Saying that she had seen her son struggle with a similar transition might have been received more in the spirit in which it was intended.

When you lack obvious common ground with the audience, appeal to higher-order and longer-term goals. Identify your "mutual purpose."[12] A mutual purpose is the most specific outcome desired by both the audience and the communicator. It may be an organizational goal, like "we all need to figure out a way to meet the growth targets the executive leadership team set" or "we both need to find ways to reduce unnecessary spending." If conflict is high, the goals might have to be even more removed from the problem, such as "we all want to figure out a path forward on this."

Frame your points around common thinking patterns

Framing provides the context that the audience uses to make meaning out of the data. Effective framing increases the impact of your communication and helps lead the audience to the right conclusions. Describing a glass as half full or half empty is an example of two different ways to frame the same phenomenon. Since framing makes meaning out of data, framing is unavoidable. The only decision you have is whether you make deliberate framing choices or inadvertent ones.

Framing doesn't change the underlying data, but it can change the decisions the audience makes based on that data. Numerous studies demonstrate this effect. In one, a fee increase for an economics conference was framed two different ways. For one group, the fee change was framed as a penalty for late registration. For another, the same change was framed as the end of a discount for early registration. When the fee change was positioned as a penalty, 93% of PhD students registered early. Only 63% did so when the fee change was positioned as a discount.[13] The only difference was the framing.

How you frame the data is one of the most important choices you make in any data communication, because framing explains what the data means.[14] Look for frames that increase comprehension, maintain the integrity of the data, and point the audience toward the appropriate conclusion. Below are four common ways to frame your data. Don't force the data into the frame. Instead, train yourself to recognize situations where certain framing techniques tend to fit the data.

---

[12] This meaning of the expression is from Kerry Patterson et al.'s *Crucial Conversations: Tools for Talking When the Stakes Are High*, an excellent read on high-stakes interpersonal communication.

[13] You would think economics PhD students would know better. The study also looked at economics faculty members. The framing did not change their registration rate. You can almost hear the study's authors—all economics faculty members—breathe a sigh of relief. As with all biases, audiences trained to recognize them can better avoid them. See S. Gächter, H. Orzen, E. Renner, and C. Stamer, "Are Experimental Economists Prone to Framing Effects? A Natural Field Experiment," *Journal of Economic Behavior and Organization* 70, no. 3 (2009): 443–446.

[14] This section merges the psychological and sociological views of framing. Framing, like persuasion, is an enormous, multidisciplinary topic that cannot be covered adequately here. I've tried to focus on a few key concepts that allow readers to start building a more nuanced understanding of its impact so they can use it to communicate data more effectively.

Personal impact > group impact > public impact

Frame the data to focus on the narrowest group with which the audience associates themselves. In individualistic cultures, this means focusing on the personal impact. In more communal cultures, this might imply a focus on the immediate work group.

Framing around the impact on a narrow group appeals to a wide variety of cognitive biases related to egocentrism: our tendency to focus on our own perspective and the difficulty we have taking others into account. A WIIFT frames the data in line with these egocentric biases. Skillfully appealing to personal impact comes with a variety of cascading benefits: it increases the chance that the audience will use the central processing route, which helps the audience muster the cognitive energy to engage with the underlying data, which leads to better understanding.

Appeals to individual impact can be uncomfortable. They force you to focus on the benefits the audience values, which may conflict with your personal values. Framing a donation as a chance to improve the donor's reputation can feel unpleasant if you believe giving should emerge from a desire to help others rather than a desire to increase one's status. But, for some audiences, the appeal to personal gain will be more effective.

Of course, no single framing works all the time. Let a realistic understanding of the audience's values guide you to the level of impact that will most resonate.

Personal impact	Group impact	Public impact
Switching to a cloud-based word processor means no more late nights merging edits from four different versions of the presentation.	Switching to a cloud-based word processor will make our group more efficient.	Switching to a cloud-based word processor will save the company $2M/year.
If we all wear personal protective equipment, the likelihood you or your loved ones will get sick is reduced by 70%.	Wearing personal protective equipment reduces the risk to the members of our team by 70%.	Wearing personal protective equipment safeguards the lives of everyone in our community.
Giving to the school's annual fund increases the value of your degree by increasing the school's standing in college rankings.	Giving to the school's annual fund helps support future students like you.	Giving to the school's annual fund helps better educate society.

Concrete > abstract

Focus on the concrete over the abstract. This means focusing the audience on benefits that can be observed with the senses rather than benefits that only exist conceptually. An abstract plan to increase "the efficiency of the team" could be framed more concretely as a plan to "get you your weekends back." Just as the most visually salient elements on a graph stand out and require less cognitive load to process, concrete images are more salient and require less cognitive load to remember.

In *Made to Stick*, Chip and Dan Heath compare memory to Velcro, with a set of hooks on one side and a set of loops on the other. Concrete images create more hooks than abstract concepts. They increase the chance that your ideas will stick in the minds of your audience.

Introducing concrete images into communications is also one of the easiest framing devices to deploy. People often resist it because the process of building expertise is one of mastering increasing levels of abstraction. Returning to the concrete can feel like sending yourself back to grade school. Remind yourself that the ability to explain complex ideas to others requires a high level of mastery, and take advantage of this technique often.

Concrete	Abstract
Using a more expensive glue will result in fewer returns from customers who call us angry that our high-end handbags smell "like chemicals."	Investing in a more expensive glue will improve our product quality.
Taking the train and working on the ride lets you spend an extra hour with your children that you used to spend working.	Taking the train to work is a more efficient use of time.
This new on-boarding process will allow us to add 300 more new customers every month without expanding the service rep team.	Improving automation in the onboarding process reduces on-boarding time by 30%.

Sooner > later

Emphasize short-term impacts even when they are less significant than longer-term ones. This effect is formally known as hyperbolic discounting. It is the well-documented phenomenon that humans tend to discount future benefits or losses well beyond what is statistically justified. The farther into the future, the stronger the effect. Audiences often prefer smaller benefits that appear sooner over larger returns which take longer to realize, even when the size of the return more than makes up for the risk of the longer time frame.

As with many of the mental shortcuts here, the strength of this effect is highly dependent on the individual and the context. With practice, individuals can develop a resistance to hyperbolic discounting, but the effect is usually limited to the domain of their expertise. Someone with experience forecasting cash flows might build exceptional intuition around the value of delayed payoffs yet still choose the satisfaction of a piece of cake today over the long-term health benefits of saying no.

Sooner	Later
If you contribute to your retirement plan now, the company will match your contributions, effectively giving you an immediate pay raise.	If you contribute to your retirement plan, the company will match your contributions, allowing you to retire more comfortably.
Hiring a full-time machine learning expert would allow us to generate $1M in cost savings within the first year, more than paying for the cost.	Hiring a full-time machine learning expert would allow us to increase revenue $230M a year by year five, more than paying for the cost.
We are going to burn half a day every week addressing this problem if we don't stop and take a full week to fix it now.	If we wait until next year, this problem will take us a month to fix.

Avoiding loss > increasing gain

When possible, frame things as a chance to hold onto what the audience already has rather than as a chance to gain more of something they don't yet have. The conference registration fee study mentioned earlier demonstrates this framing. When the price change was framed as a loss, PhD students acted to avoid losing out on the lower price they already had. When the initial price was framed as a discount to the "real" price, students were less motivated to increase their gain and capture the same savings.

This aversion to loss is among the most well-documented cognitive biases.[15] We are more likely to protect what we already have than we are to take steps to improve our position, even when the likely gains well outweigh the risks. The pain of losing a hundred dollars is greater than the joy of winning the same amount.

Use this simple insight to open up opportunities for framing. Take advantage of it when inaction is an option for your audience. Use it to frame your findings around the costs of inaction rather than the benefits of action.

Avoiding loss	Increasing gain
If we don't enter this new market, the competition could beat us to it.	Entering this new market could help grow the company.
A new lead scoring system could help us win 5% of the leads we currently lose.	A new lead scoring system could help increase our sales win rate by 5%.
Offering a good training program will reduce the number of candidates who reject our job offer.	Offering a good training program will increase the quality of our applicant pool.

---

[15] On its "List of cognitive biases" page, Wikipedia lists over a hundred biases related to decision-making. Some favorites include:
- The "rhyme as reason effect" in which we tend to find rhyming statements more truthful
- The "Ikea effect" where we tend to overvalue things we assemble ourselves, even if the work is poor
- The "Google effect" where we tend to forget information that can be easily retrieved via search engines
- The "picture superiority effect" when concepts learned visually are more easily learned than concepts presented in text

"List of Cognitive Biases," Wikipedia, last modified August 15, 2020, https://en.wikipedia.org/wiki/List_of_cognitive_biases

Key concepts from this chapter

How you frame the data impacts how the audience interprets it. Make sure you know What's In It For Them (WIIFT) to maximize their engagement.

THE PERSUASION CHECKLIST

Have you	Maximize your persuasive power
Established What's In It For Them (WIIFT)?	• Who is your audience? • What impact will this have on this audience? • Why does this data matter to this audience?
Established the source of your credibility?	• Does your rank increase your credibility with this audience? • Is the audience aware of your legitimate expertise? • Have you invested in generating goodwill with this audience? • Have you identified the common ground you share with this audience?
Framed your points in the most persuasive way possible?	• Can you identify a more personal impact on this audience? • Can you provide concrete examples and metaphors? • Can you identify a short-term impact that will resonate? • Can you frame your point around avoiding loss?

If you remember nothing else . . .

The highest-impact thing you can do in any business communication is to identify "What's In It For Them"—the WIIFT—for the audience.

Plan to craft a new WIIFT for every audience, even if it's the only thing you change about your communication.

Despite your best efforts, expect most audiences to use peripheral processing most of the time.

Don't look to manipulate the data, look for the framing that will maximize the data's impact on the audience.

Exercise: Making the case at Craigstone—Part II

Create a different Minto pyramid for each audience described in the scenarios below. Focus your main idea around a WIIFT that would appeal to that audience. Make reasonable assumptions about what each audience would care about. Adjust your key points and supporting evidence to support your new main idea. Use the facts from "Making the case at Craigstone—Part I" in the previous chapter.

Scenario 1: The founding partners

You are the analyst on the committee. You and the chair of the committee have done most of the analysis and have decided that CanEx is the best choice for the firm. The chair has asked you to present the findings and recommendation to the other four partners on the committee.

All five of the partners on the committee have been at the firm since its founding thirty years ago. Three of them are in their later sixties, and the rumor is that they will retire soon. Building this firm has been the most significant accomplishment of their careers. They consider its continued health their personal and professional legacy. During the research process, one partner asked you to show her how to book a flight on her phone. She commented that the last time she personally booked any travel was 1999, right before they hired a full-time assistant for her.

Scenario 2: The junior partners

You are the analyst on the committee. You and the chair of the committee have done most of the analysis and have decided that CanEx is the best choice for the firm. The chair has asked you to present the findings and recommendation to the other four partners on the committee.

Most of the partners on the committee are in their late thirties, and all of them were promoted to partner within the last three years. The rumor within the firm is that membership on the committee is both a privilege and a burden. Only partners recognized as rising stars were asked to participate. The firm policy is that new partners have five years to prove their ability to sell new business, or they are asked to leave the firm. These meetings represent time that could be spent cultivating relationships with existing clients and pursuing new ones. In every meeting you've attended, most of the committee members are on their phones for most of the meeting.

Scenario 3: The future firm leader

You are the chair of the travel policy committee and the most senior partner on the committee. Working with the analyst, you've determined that CanEx is the best choice for the firm. You are addressing the other partners on the committee to get them to approve your choice.

In the past year, you were responsible for 20% of the firm's revenue, more than any other partner. You are in line to be the next leader of the entire firm. Since you are on the partner promotion committee, you know all the other partners on the committee well and were involved in their promotions to partner. You consider two of them to be protégés. You hope to see them become the future leaders of the firm (after you).

You asked to head this committee because you run the relationship with the firm's largest client. After the client's CEO threatened to end its relationship with Craigstone, you promised that you would get travel costs under control. You're convinced that runaway travel costs are going to limit the ability of the firm to sell projects to other Fortune 100 companies. Over the years, you've seen clients focus more and more on travel expenses. You are tired of taking calls from third-year accountants just to ask you about a Sam Adams some twenty-two-year-old expensed on a 10 p.m. flight back to Boston after a week in Omaha.

Scenario 4: The analyst meeting

You are the analyst on the committee. The committee has recommended the firm adopt CanEx as the company's official charge card, and the full partnership has approved the decision. Since you were on the committee, the partners have asked you to explain the decision to select CanEx at the Boston office's analyst meeting. Presenting at this meeting is an honor and a signal that you have a bright future within the firm.

The committee chair implied that your real job is to convince your peers to adopt and use their CanEx credit cards for all business expenses. The firm's official policy is that only charges on CanEx cards are reimbursed, but no one believes it. The announcement was buried in a monthly email newsletter, and partners have been telling their teams that no one is going to make someone one year out of school shoulder the cost of a $3,000 business trip, regardless of the card it goes on. Besides, gaming credit card offers and points programs is considered both a common hobby and one of the job's perks. It helps make up for the punishing amount of travel required.

There are twenty other analysts in the Boston office. You are generally on good terms with all of them, but your close relationships with partners on the committee has caused some jealousy. Being the one to explain the policy doesn't seem like it will help your reputation as a sycophant.

Scenario 5: The analyst lunch

You are the analyst on the committee. The committee has recommended that the firm adopt CanEx as the official charge card of the company, and the full partnership has approved the decision. The monthly email newsletter contained an announcement of the policy, but the meetings to explain the policy don't start until next week.

It's one of those rare Fridays where everyone is in the office. All the analysts who started with you at Craigstone try to get lunch together whenever most of you are around. If you can get to Aceituna—the Middle Eastern place around the corner—before 11:45, you can usually assemble enough tables for all eight of you to sit together.

When you're midway through your shawarma, someone asks, "So what's the deal with this CanEx nonsense? First this job steals my evenings and weekends, now they're taking my credit card perks. Is this because the partners who have assistants to do everything for them can't even figure out how to book a hotel room on their phones?" As you put down your pita, you notice that all the side conversations at the table have stopped. Everyone is looking at you.

Part IV

Delivering and Defending Your Data

—

How to prepare for and respond to your audience

CHAPTER 8

Present Your Data
(with less preparation)

—

IF YOU KEEP SAYING "BEAR WITH ME FOR A MOMENT", PEOPLE TAKE A WHILE TO FIGURE OUT THAT YOU'RE JUST SHOWING THEM RANDOM SLIDES.

Source: https://xkcd.com/365

Despite the common expression, data does not speak for itself. Data can't talk, and it certainly can't explain its implications for your audience. This chapter transitions from a focus on creating your communication to tools that help you present your findings in front of an audience. It explains how to give your data a voice. The first half of the chapter outlines the TOP-T framework, an approach to presenting individual data-oriented slides. Mastering this framework will help you clarify the meaning of the data, accelerate your audience's understanding, and increase your persuasive power. The second half of the chapter goes into advanced presentation techniques. The exercise provides practice slides to help you sharpen your skills.

Give your data a voice

At their best, data-oriented presentations allow you to facilitate interactions that yield rich discussions and result in good decisions. At their worst, data presentations devolve into a defensive scramble. You end up apologizing for the limits of the methodology, and the audience walks away with the belief that the data is meaningless or irrelevant.

Having a good framework for presenting individual data slides is a formula for avoiding this mess. Going through data slides with a repeated structure helps you consistently meet audience needs. The TOP-T framework presented here makes sure you cover all the important elements of a good presentation and aligns your content with the audience's mental processing patterns. Unlike the Minto pyramid, which plans your whole communication at a macro level, the TOP-T framework is a micro tool. It covers how to present an individual data slide within a presentation. Using it builds the audience's trust in the data, their confidence in your ability to interpret it, and everyone's capacity to engage in a productive discussion.

Use the TOP-T framework to guide your audience

The TOP-T framework consists of the four verbal elements the audience needs from the presenter to process every data slide: the Topic, the Orient, the Point, and the Transition.[1] The section below describes each element at a high level followed by a deep dive on each component. When presenting slides, make sure to cover the following four elements on every slide:

The Topic: Share the two or three words that introduce the topic of the slide. Say them before showing the slide to help snap the audience into the right context before the onslaught of visual information that comes with every slide transition.

The Orient: Narrate the audience's visual journey through every encoding on the graph. Talk them through each axis, the data, the analysis, acronyms, the methodology, and any calculations. This should be the longest—and is the most important—part of the presentation. An effective orient helps the audience understand your data and allows them to verify your conclusions for themselves.

The Point: State the key point of the graph. It should also be the headline of the slide. If you oriented properly, the point should be quick, and the audience should think, "Of course! That's what the data shows." After the point, you can pause for questions or discussion.

The Transition: Connect the content on this slide to the content of the next slide. Effective transitions build a story by linking the slides to each other and placing them within the context of the entire presentation. Humans connect ideas and look for patterns, even when they aren't there. Tell your audience how the ideas connect so they don't create connections that aren't there. Effective transitions incorporate the topic of the next slide.

---

[1] There are as many variants of this framework as there are attempts to codify a data-presentation framework. Though the ordering and emphasis changes, every approach tends to include similar themes. This one is adapted from frameworks I encountered at the consulting firm Bain & Company in the early 2000s. This approach has been validated over decades of work with professionals across a variety of organizations, industries, and levels of seniority.

Master each component of the TOP-T framework

The next section breaks down each component of TOP-T using the slide below. Each component has examples, common mistakes, and signs that a component has been performed well.

Assume that the intended audience for this slide and graph is the leadership team of a medium-sized division within a larger company. In this scenario, everyone on the team is familiar with sales data, but some team members review it only once a quarter.

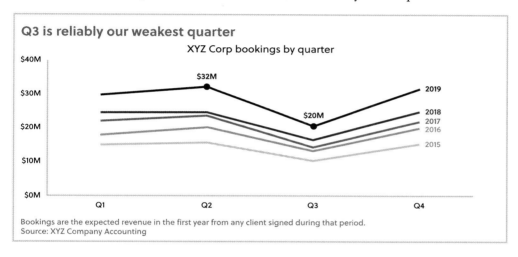

A sample presentation script using TOP-T	
Topic	"Let's look at patterns in quarterly booked revenue"[2]
Orient	"This shows booked revenue by quarter for the last four years, from 2015 on the bottom to 2019 on top. As a reminder, bookings are the total revenue we expect over the next year from all the customers the sales team closed in that quarter. For example, if a new customer signs up in Q1 for a year-long contract with $1M paid every quarter, we book $4M from that client in Q1. "In 2019, customers closed in Q2 were expected to generate $32M in revenue over the next year. In Q3 we only closed customers worth $20M over the next year. The same Q3 dip has occurred every year for the past five years."
Point	"Our business is seasonal, and Q3 is reliably our weakest quarter."
Transition	"We explored the reasons why bookings decline in Q3."

Using the example slide, let's dive into each element of the TOP-T framework.

1. Preview the topic

The topic is the brief description of what type of data the slide shows. The topic should be a few words and avoid jumping to the conclusion of the data. It describes the kind of data being presented, such as "revenue" or "an analysis of customer profitability."

The graph title is also the slide's topic.

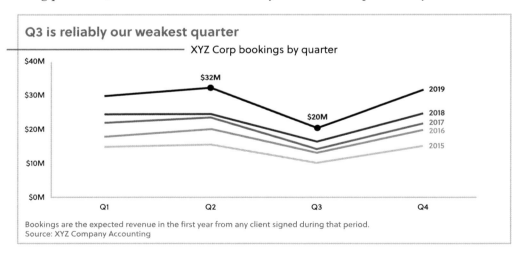

Q3 is reliably our weakest quarter

XYZ Corp bookings by quarter

Bookings are the expected revenue in the first year from any client signed during that period.
Source: XYZ Company Accounting

---

[2] The audience's familiarity would determine the level of detail required to define bookings. As a general rule, if anyone in the audience doesn't work with this metric as part of their regular job function and is involved in decisions that this data informs, err on the side of more explanation rather than less, as this example does.

The topic snaps the audience into the context of the slide and speeds their digestion of the content. When a new slide flashes onscreen or a page turns, a wave of new information washes over an audience. Stating the topic helps ease that transition and provides a moment to refocus the wandering minds in the audience. Take careful advantage of this moment.

Example topics for this slide
- "We looked at bookings ..."
- "First, we considered bookings ..."
- "Let's look at bookings ..."

The most common topic mistake is ...
Starting with the point of the slide. The audience needs time to decode the graph. Allow them time to understand what they are seeing and come to the conclusion your data lays out for themselves. If you share the conclusion before the audience has had time to process the slide, you risk triggering people's reflexive instinct to challenge anything they don't fully understand. You also turn yourself into the focus of their challenge rather than centering the data.

You'll know it's working when ...
Your transition from the previous slide and the topic for this slide merge together.

> **WATCH OUT: Focus on the what the data shows, not what "the graph shows"**
>
> Avoid the phrase "the graph shows." Focus the audience on the underlying data, not how it's visualized. It's not the graph that shows your business is seasonal. It's the data underlying that graph. If you find yourself relying on this phrase often, try instead to emphasize the source of the data. For example, "sales trends confirm that our business is seasonal."

2. Orient the audience

Orient the audience by narrating them through every encoding on a data slide. This is the most important step in effective data presentations. Many presenters fear that a detailed orient patronizes the audience. This fear allows you to avoid the more terrifying truth: your audience probably isn't listening to you very carefully, or at all. Even if they are in the same room, even if they are looking right at you, there's still no guarantee they are paying attention.[3] Fully orient the audience to help them understand the graph. That understanding will drive acceptance of your conclusions.

---

[3] Just ask any classroom teacher or self-aware student.

While it is possible to over-orient, the overwhelming default is toward under-orienting. Remember that the Curse of Knowledge tends to blind you to the audience's experience. You have spent much more time thinking about this data than the audience has. Give them time to process everything.

Orient to
- X-axis
- Y-axis
- Lines
- Bookings definition
- Specific examples

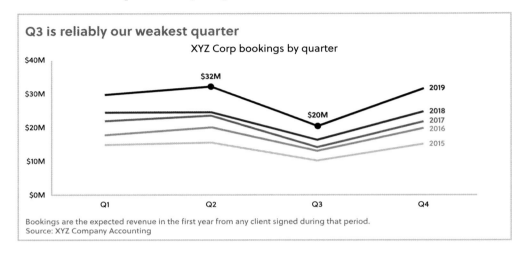

The orient checklist

When orienting, think about narrating and explaining every element of the graph. Imagine a mental checklist of all the elements on the graph. If your graphs are well formed, all these elements should be labeled for easy reference. They usually include:

- The x-axis
- The y-axis
- All the different ways the graph encodes variables, such as the height of the bars, shapes, and hues for categories and any reference lines or markers
- Terms or acronyms any member of the audience might not immediately understand
- The filter you used to select which data to show, such as "the top 5 sales performers"
- Any aggregation or calculations you have done, such as averages, regressions, or rate calculations
- Any relevant methodology or assumptions used to generate the elements this slide graphs
- One specific example point to help clarify the data

Example orients for this slide

Creating an orient that is both succinct and covers every element requires practice. Below are two versions of an orient for this slide. The first suggests how an orient might sound for someone reading the elements off the slide. The second version suggests how a more practiced orient might sound.

With limited time to prepare, use the graph elements to guide you	With more time to prepare, walk the audience through the slide without having to name every graphical element
"On the x-axis we're showing each quarter of the year. On the y-axis is the booked revenue in that quarter."	"This shows the seasonality of booked revenue by quarter for the last four years, from 2015 on the bottom to the most recent year, 2019, on top."
"Booked revenue is the total of the first year of revenue we expect from all the clients the sales team closed in that quarter."	"Bookings are the total revenue we expect for the next year from all the customers the sales team closed in that quarter. For example, if a new client signs up in Q1 for a year-long contract with $1M paid every quarter, the bookings for that client are $4M in Q1."
"The top line is the most recent year: 2019. The lines go from the most recent year at the top to least recent year at the bottom. In 2019, for example, we have bookings of $32M in Q2 and $20M in Q3."	"In 2019, customers closed in Q2 were expected to generate $32M in revenue over the next year. The customers closed in Q3 are only expected to generate $20M over the next year. The same Q3 dip has occurred every year for the past 5 years."

The most common orienting mistake is . . .

Either spending too little time orienting or skipping the orient entirely and going straight to the point before the audience has had time to process the graph.

You know it's working when . . .

All of the audience's questions are predictable and on topic.

Irrelevant, off-topic questions or unexpected challenges to the conclusion are signs that the audience needed more orientation earlier in the presentation. Note when other presenters fail to orient and how it leads to audience confusion and off-topic comments on later slides.

WATCH OUT: Skipping the Orient leaves audiences disoriented

Two human traits conspire to make presenting data challenging:

- Audiences are unable to process conflicting visual and auditory information simultaneously.
- Presenters suffer from the Curse of Knowledge and can't remember what it is like to be unfamiliar with this data.

The brain processes audio and visual information through two different channels. As a visual species, most people tend to favor the visual channel and tune out the auditory channel when the information from each channel conflicts. These conflicts occur often when the audience is still visually decoding a graph but the presenter has moved on to explain what the slide means. In these cases, audience members tend to ignore the auditory channel and miss hearing the point of the slide. Alternatively, when the images we see and the words we hear line up, our ability to incorporate that information into future decisions increases by as much as 30%.[4]

Narrating your audience through a slide helps align the audience's visual and auditory input. It also forces the presenter to start from where the audience is, walking through every element of the slide as if seeing it for the first time or having only briefly looked at it beforehand.

WATCH OUT: Stay specific

It is easy for humans to generalize from specific details and difficult to create specific examples based on general statements.[5] For example, if you know that someone leaves their desk empty overnight except for a pad of paper and a single pen always lined up with the center left side of that pad, you might generalize that this is probably the desk of a very organized person. In contrast, if you know that someone is organized, it's hard to describe what their desk looks like. This is also why concrete images and ideas tend to have more staying power in our memories.

Take advantage of this trait by describing a single data point on each graph in order to clarify the underlying comparison for the audience. In the example slide, the comparison of the Q2 and Q3 bookings serves this purpose and focuses the audience's attention on the most recent year.

---

[4] This is a distillation of Richard Mayer's work on multimedia learning. In experiments, Mayer and his colleagues usually separated verbal and visual descriptions in time, space, or form (narration vs. words on screen). In one experiment, subjects watched a video showing how brakes and pumps work followed by a verbal explanation of the same topic. They were then were asked to complete tasks that measured how well they had internalized the explanation. Over eight experiments that varied whether verbal and visual information were presented together or sequentially, presenting the verbal and visual information simultaneously had a median effect size of 1.3 on retention of the information. There do not appear to be any experiments that replicate the presentation experience of a speaker talking about future implications of a process while the audience views visuals explaining the process. It seems safe to assume the results would be poor. See Richard E. Mayer and Roxana Moreno, "Nine Ways to Reduce Cognitive Load in Multimedia Learning," *Educational Psychologist* 38, no. 1 (2003): 43–52.

[5] This concept is an illustration of both (1) the power of concrete ideas and (2) our resistance to applying statistical generalizations to specific cases. See Mark Sadoski et al., "Engaging Texts: Effects of Concreteness on Comprehensibility, Interest, and Recall in Four Text Types," *Journal of Educational Psychology* 92, no. 1 (January 2000): 85–95; Richard E. Nisbett and Eugene Borgida, "Attribution and the Psychology of Prediction," *Journal of Personality and Social Psychology* 32 (November 1975): 932–943.

3. Make the point

The point is the reason why this audience needs to understand this data. It is the explicit statement of what the data shows. Ideally, it is a clear, brief implication of the visualization. In a well-written and well-designed slide, the written headline of the slide is also the verbal point of the slide. Don't be afraid to repeat it word for word.

When you get to your point, aspire to have the audience think, "Of course! That's what this data clearly shows."

The place for questions and discussion of this data is after the point.

Example points for this slide
- "Q3 is reliably our weakest quarter."
- "Our business is seasonal with a weak Q3."
- "Our business is seasonal, and Q3 is reliably our weakest quarter."

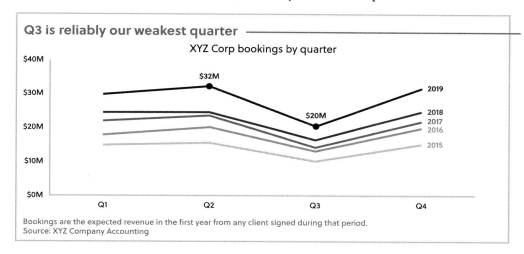

The headline is the slide's point.

The most common point mistake is . . .

Making a point that goes beyond the data on the slide. On the example slide, saying, "We need to invest in more sales promotions during Q3" would go beyond what this data shows. The only thing this slide establishes is that seasonality exists. The audience still needs more information to demonstrate what the corrective action, if any, should be.[6]

---

[6] As discussed in chapter 5, there are cases in which the audience will agree to conclusions that go beyond the data on the slide. These leaps from data to action work when the audience and presenter share a preexisting mental model about the cause-and-effect relationships at work in this situation. If an audience thinks seasonal variation is a problem and that sales promotions are the most effective tool to combat seasonal dips, they might agree to invest in Q3 sales promotions on this evidence alone. Perhaps there were discussions before the formal presentation, and there is already consensus around next steps. Just because an audience accepts your conclusion about how to respond to this data, it's not necessarily because this evidence made a strong case for that particular course of action. Many factors influence an audience's decision to take action.

You know it's working when . . .

The audience accepts the point and moves straight to discussing the implications of the data and the actions that follow from it.

> **WATCH OUT: If you have to tell the audience something is clear to see, assume it's not**
>
> Avoid the phrase "as you can see" and its even worse cousin "as you can *clearly* see." If you have to inform the audience that they are able to see something, consider whether it is really that easy to see. If you find yourself using this phrase, double check to make sure your point is as clear as you think it is.

4. Transition clearly

The transition is the statement that connects the current slide to the next slide. It should be said before advancing the slide. Remember that every slide change floods the audience with new information. Effective transitions ease the cognitive load of that deluge. The transition signals that the presenter is moving on and primes the audience for the new information they are about to see.

Some common transitions

Any logical connection can form the basis for transition. Some common ones include:

- **Transitions in time:** "Those were our results for Q3. In Q4 we saw . . ."
- **Steps in a process:** "Errors in picking tend to compound when we move to the next step: packing . . ."
- **Performing the same analysis on a different group:** "Heavy users consume the product differently than our occasional users . . ."
- **Performing a different analysis on the same group:** "First-time buyers may purchase at the same time of day as repeat users, but they buy very different things . . ."
- **Zooming in:** "Q4 is our strongest quarter, but the picture looks different when we break it down by month . . ."
- **Zooming out:** "The sales behavior we see in California isn't reflective of the entire West Coast . . ."

Example transitions for this slide

- "Let's look at why sales reliably decline in the 3rd quarter."
- "Why do sales keep declining in Q3?"
- "We considered many approaches to address this decline."

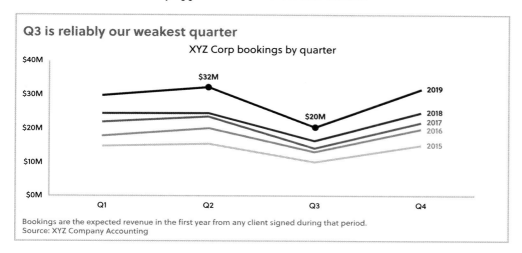

Q3 is reliably our weakest quarter

XYZ Corp bookings by quarter

Bookings are the expected revenue in the first year from any client signed during that period.
Source: XYZ Company Accounting

Transition to connect to the next slide.

The most common transition mistake is . . .

Advancing to the next the slide before the transition or without a clear transition.

You know it's working when . . .

The audience's questions set up the transition to the next slide. This is a sign that you have built a clear, logical story.[7]

WATCH OUT: Present multigraph slides as if they are multiple slides

When a multigraph slide is appropriate, think of each graph as its own slide. Fully orient to one graph, make the point of that graph, and then transition to the next graph. Avoid jumping back and forth between the two graphs during the orient. If you are presenting digitally, consider animating each graph so that the second graph doesn't appear until after you orient the first graph and share the point. When the graphs are connected, clarify which elements from the second graph are repeated from the first graph. For example: *"The graph on the right looks at revenue over the same time period as the graph on the left, but divides it by region rather than product . . ."*

---

[7] It's also emotionally satisfying when someone asks a question, and you get to advance the slide to present the answer to their question.

Practice some advanced techniques

Avoid the "ta-da!"

It can be tempting to surprise the audience with the point of the slide, especially when you conducted the analysis. There was a moment when the finding was a surprise to you. It's natural to want to share your excitement with the audience. Remember that part of your excitement was the confirmation that you had analyzed data effectively and derived insight from it. Don't deny the audience the satisfaction of experiencing that feeling themselves. Slow down and allow the audience to go through the process of interpreting the data and coming to the same conclusion you did.

Presenters who take that moment away from the audience and claim it for themselves risk triggering audience members' well-trained instinct to challenge any point or conclusion they did not arrive at themselves. Sharing the point as a big reveal also risks moving on before an audience has full clarity. Audience members are rarely brave enough to raise a hand and say, "I'm sorry. I know this is a simple line graph, and I've worked here for five years, but I don't fully understand the concept of bookings." Instead, they challenge your other conclusions.

If the headline is clear, the orient is complete, and the analysis is sound, take silent pride in the knowledge that your good analysis, effective slide design, and clear orient have led the audience to the right conclusion.

Know when to start with the point

The TOP-T framework can appear to contradict the advice given in writing classes and even elsewhere in this book to start with the point. Starting with the point is good advice for the overall structure of your presentation but not great advice for individual data slides.

When sharing the overview of the communication, use the structure you developed with your Minto pyramid to preview the overall logic of your presentation at the start and the logic of each section at its beginning.

When getting into a slide that presents your evidence, let the audience come to a full understanding of the data before you share the point. Allow people to absorb the data so that they can confirm for themselves that it supports the conclusions shared earlier in the presentation.

There are times where it is appropriate to begin each slide with the point. Some audiences may demand it.[8] If the audience demands it, do it. More generally, start with the point when the audience meets all four of the following tests:

- They are familiar with the specific graph type you are using.
- They are familiar with the exact analysis you have conducted (usually because they see it regularly).
- They trust the data source.
- They believe you are credible and trustworthy.

Consider the silent orient

If the graph is exceptionally well-designed and the data is familiar to the audience, consider the silent orient. Instead of orienting the audience verbally, transition the slide and silently count to a very slow five before sharing the point. This is an advanced move that requires both flawless slide design and exceptional presenter discipline. Consider this advanced move only when all of the following are true:

- The graph is well designed with a clear, visually salient point.
- All the data choices on the graph are explained on the slide.
- The font and data density are scaled for the environment—for example, every element of the slide is readable from the back seat of the conference room.
- The graph type is familiar to every member of the audience.

---

[8] Early in my career, I had one boss who could process visual information at stunning speed. I think she had seen and internalized every conceivable way of analyzing and displaying business data. The ideal way to communicate with her was to sit in silent awe for a few minutes while she inhaled a printed version of your presentation, then marvel at her ability to zero in on the weakest assumption in a thirty-page analysis.

Key concepts from this chapter

Use the TOP-T framework to minimize cognitive load on your audience, maximize clarity, and reduce your preparation time.

THE GRAPH PRESENTATION CHECKLIST

Have you	Check your TOP-T outline
Identified the topic of this slide?	• Does the topic align with the title of the graph?
Oriented the audience to every element of the graph?	• Have you explained the x- and y-axes? • Have you explained all the encodings on the graph? • Have you explained any terms or acronyms anyone in the audience might be unfamiliar with? • Have you explained the filter you used to select this data? • Have you explained all the calculations and assumptions? • Have you explained the methodology? • Have you provided a specific example to help clarify what the audience is seeing?
Shared the point of the slide?	• Have you made sure the headline is the point of the slide? • Have you remembered to say the point clearly after the orient?
Transitioned to the next slide?	• Have you connected the point of this slide to the next slide? • Have you embedded the topic of the next slide in your transition? • Have you shared the transition before advancing to the next slide?

If you remember nothing else . . .

The data cannot speak for itself. You have to give it a voice.

Orient. Orient. Orient.

Avoid the "ta-da." After the point, the audience should think, "Of course! That's what this data clearly shows."

Even if they are in the same room, even if they are looking right at you, there's still no guarantee they are paying attention.

Exercise: Practice presenting

Your team has just handed you one of the slides below, and you have to present to your company's senior leadership team in five minutes. Take a moment to:

- Write down the topic.
- Circle all the elements on each graph to which you want to orient the audience.
- Decide if the headline given is an appropriate point. If not, write a better point.
- Write out the transition to a hypothetical next slide (you can choose whatever content you want to come next).

Then present the slide as if you support all the design choices. Remember, in real life you won't always have time to craft the perfect slide. Use this as a chance to practice presenting with confidence. Lack of confidence in delivery can accidentally signal lack of confidence in the analysis. Practice displaying confidence in the analysis through confidence in the delivery.

To improve faster, record yourself and play it back. Ask yourself the following questions to make sure you are presenting the slide clearly:

1. How clear was your topic?
2. To which elements of the graph did you orient? Which ones did you miss? What terms or choices warranted more explanation?
3. How could you have stated the point more clearly?
4. How could you have improved the transition to the next slide?

Compare your choices to the sample scripts after the slides. Notice what you like about the sample scripts. Notice where you think they could be improved. There's no one way to present a slide. Cultivate a sense of what you think works by observing other people's choices.

Practice Slide 1

Assume the audience for this slide is facilities leadership at a company based in New England with multiple comparably sized facilities all in that region.

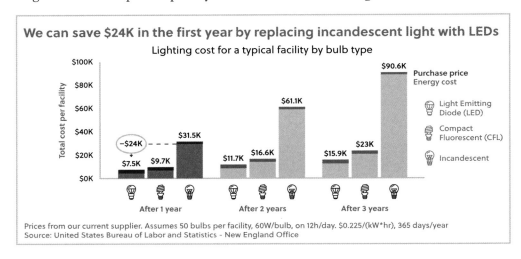

Practice Slide 2

Assume that you are delivering this slide in 2018 at a company that provides services to the US military.

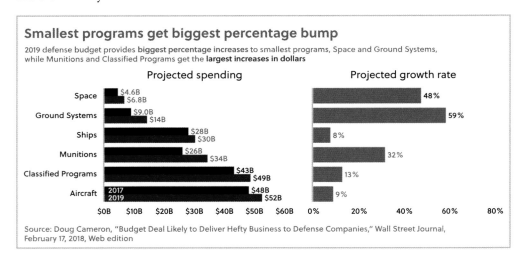

Practice Slide 3: Try a more complex graph

Use complex graphs when the underlying data is complex and the complexity is critical to your point.

For the slide below, it's important to know that RPK (Revenue Passenger Kilometers) is a measure of airline activity. It measures the number of paying passengers (revenue passengers) multiplied by the number of kilometers they flew. An airline that runs a single 1,000-kilometer flight with 100 passengers has an RPK of 100,000 (1 flight × 1,000 Km × 100 passengers). An airline that carries 200 passengers twice as far has an RPK of 400,000 (1 flight × 2,000 Km × 200 passengers).

Assume that you are delivering this slide in 2015 and practice the discipline of fully orienting the audience to every element and calculation on the slide.

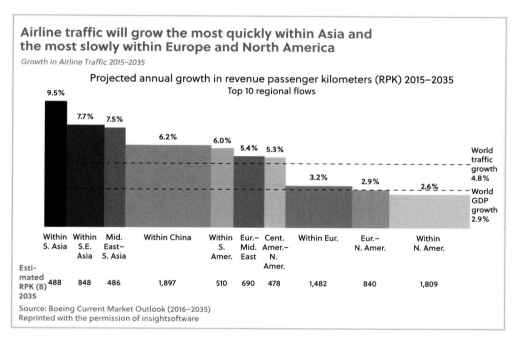

Sample scripts

Topic	"The savings from switching to LEDs could be substantial."
Orient	"We've graphed the average costs to light our facilities with LED, CFL, and incandescent bulbs over one, two, and three years. The two components of lighting cost are the purchase price of the bulbs themselves in burgundy and the energy to power the bulbs in gray. The full cost of the bulb is included in the calculation at every time period. In the first year alone . . ."
Point	". . . we save an average of $24K if we convert from incandescent bulbs to LEDs, even accounting for the cost of the bulbs."
Transition	"The savings are still substantial when we include the cost of the labor it will take to make the switch . . ."

Practice Slide 2

1st graph (on the left)

Topic	"Let's look at the budget changes for the US military."
Orient	"On the left is a comparison of 2017 US military spending by program compared to the projected 2019 spending based on the most recent budget passed by the US Congress. For example, aircraft spending, the largest line item, will increase from $48B to $52B with the most recent budget."
Point	"Congress authorized increased spending on every major program . . ."
Transition	"But the increases are not evenly distributed." (transition to 2nd graph)

2nd graph (on the right)

Topic	"Some programs have much larger percentage increases."
Orient	"On the right are the percentage increases in spending for each program. The budget for the military Space program increased by 48%."
Point	"Space and Ground Systems, the two smallest programs, will grow much faster than the larger programs."
Transition	"For our industry, that means we need to consider a change in how we allocate resources."

Topic	"We've displayed our projections for airline traffic growth over the next twenty years."
Orient	"This slide displays the current size of the market on the x-axis and its projected growth rate on the y-axis.
	"The measure of market size on the x-axis is Revenue Passenger Kilometers, called RPK. This is the airline industry's primary measure of air traffic. One paying passenger, a revenue passenger, traveling one kilometer, is 1 RPK. Airlines can increase RPK by carrying more passengers per flight, adding flights, or flying longer distances.
	"Here the width of each region is the current RPK for each region in 2015.
	"The height is the projected growth for that region through 2035.
	"So, the area is the total RPK for that region in 2035, which is shown below each region.
	"For example, China is starting from a slightly smaller base than North America but will grow an average 6.2% per year compared to North American growth of 2.6% per year. By 2035 China's RKP of 1,897B is projected to be slightly larger than North America's 1,809B.
	"For comparison, the world GDP growth during the same time is 2.9% and overall airline traffic growth is 4.8%. Comparing the Asian regions' growth in burgundy with the American and European regions' growth in yellow and teal . . ."
Point	"We project that while North America and Europe are currently larger markets, most of the industry's growth will come from Asia."
Transition	"The drivers of that growth are a combination of adding routes and flying larger airplanes."

CHAPTER 9

Prepare for Resistance

(because resistance shows they care)

——

ALL SPORTS COMMENTARY

Eventually, every communicator meets with resistance from their audience. This chapter explains how to better anticipate and prepare for the kinds of challenges you are likely to encounter. It discusses how to think about the nature of change so that you can better predict your audience's behavior, and it introduces the Audience Confusion Matrix so that you can prepare an appropriate response. The final section of the chapter provides some strategies for defusing difficult situations. The exercise offers a chance to predict the audience's response to different scenarios and think through the appropriate preparation.

Resistance can be productive

Audiences challenge communicators because that's what they are trained to do. Higher education across almost every discipline cultivates the ability to evaluate other people's data and arguments critically. In the workplace, meaningful rewards accrue to those who demonstrate these skills. Those rewards may feel well deserved when they support a culture that holds people to high standards in pursuit of making better decisions. Those rewards may feel unfair when they elevate people who dismantle the work of others in order to avoid positive change and undermine others with displays of intellectual superiority.

These toxic environments—real or imagined—often lead communicators to fear audience resistance to their analysis. Believing that fewer questions signal better presentations and that more data reduces audience resistance, communicators clutter up graphs and add needless details to protect themselves from challenges. They mistake low resistance from an audience for high acceptance of their conclusions. Don't fall prey to these fallacies. Resistance shows that the audience cares. It is one of the few ways you can know for certain that your audience is engaged.

Mentally reframe resistance from your audience as a unique opportunity to capitalize on their engagement. The Audience Confusion Matrix presented here will help you anticipate how an audience will react to your analysis and how you can turn challenges into a chance to increase your credibility. If the audience feels that their concerns have been heard and addressed, their commitment to your conclusions will increase.

Also, if you do this well, people will think you are very smart.

Resistance can be predicted

To understand how audiences will react to analyses that describe existing phenomena or predict future phenomena, you have to understand how audiences experience change and how they react to new information. The following simple guidelines will help you evaluate an audience's likely response to your analysis:

1. Audiences react to changes in ratios, not changes in values.
2. Audiences react to changes in their internal expectations, not changes in the external world.

Audiences react to changes in ratios, not changes in values

People react to change. If nothing has changed, people are unlikely to react. So, understanding an audience's reaction requires that you understand what constitutes change. People are much more likely to react to changes in the ratio at which a phenomenon occurs than they are to react to changes in measures of its value.

Take the following example. It uses ones of the most common types of ratios: a growth rate.[1] Imagine you are in year 3. What would year 4 sales look like if "nothing changed"?

CONSTANT RATES LOOK LIKE NO CHANGE

Revenue

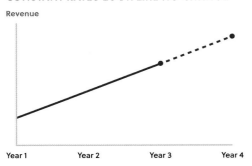

| Year 1 | Year 2 | Year 3 | Year 4 |

CHANGES IN RATE LOOK LIKE REAL CHANGE

Revenue

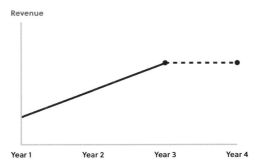

| Year 1 | Year 2 | Year 3 | Year 4 |

(Left) If sales continue to grow at the *same rate*, audiences *do not* experience this as a change.

(Right) If sales stay at the *same value*, audiences tend to experience this as a *large change*.

If revenue continued to grow at the same rate into year 4, it would not feel like anything had fundamentally changed. Though the growth in sales might require the organization to hire more people or change some processes, the company's underlying situation would feel unchanged.

Compare that to a situation where sales stay flat from year 3 to year 4. In this situation the value being measured is unchanged. It's the same from year 3 to year 4, but the

---

[1] A rate is a type of ratio that compares two numbers with the same unit.

audience would experience this as a profound change for the company. Any CEO who told their board of directors that "nothing changed" from year 3 to year 4 because revenue stayed the same ought to prepare for a rapid change in their employment situation. This is because audiences respond to changes in ratios, not changes in value.

Since time series graphs visualize change over time, changes in rate are easiest to identify in these types of comparisons. Detecting changes in one-time measurements requires you to express measurements as ratios to spot real underlying changes.

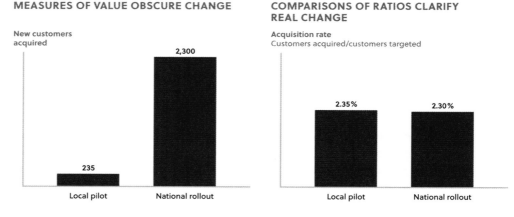

MEASURES OF VALUE OBSCURE CHANGE

New customers acquired

2,300

235

Local pilot   National rollout

COMPARISONS OF RATIOS CLARIFY REAL CHANGE

Acquisition rate
Customers acquired/customers targeted

2.35%   2.30%

Local pilot   National rollout

(Left) Measured by value, the national rollout was more successful than the pilot.

(Right) Measured by ratio, it's clear that the national campaign performed as the pilot predicted it would.

For example, a national marketing campaign that yields 2,300 customers may feel like a big win for a team who worked hard to scale up a local pilot program that drew only 235 customers. The actual success of the campaign, however, depends on the ratio, not the absolute value. By expressing the campaign results as ratios, it's easier to tell if the results of the national campaign represent a change in performance or just a change in scale. If the pilot targeted 10,000 prospects and the national campaign targeted 100,000 prospects—10× more—then both campaigns performed on par with each other. The pilot converted 2.35% of prospects to customers and the national campaign converted 2.30%. Accounting for reasonable margins of error, there was no change in the performance of the campaign as it scaled from pilot to national. The lack of difference is obvious when the campaign's performance is expressed as a ratio. When it's not, expect audiences to explicitly press you on the change in ratio or implicitly sense a gap in your analysis.

Understanding that audiences react to changes in ratios helps you understand how the audience will respond to your analysis. Prepare more carefully when presenting data that describes changes in ratios, because audiences react more strongly to these changes. In those situations, expect your audience to be more likely to question the data, the analysis, and the analyst.

Audiences react to changes in their internal expectations, not changes in the external world

People react to information that challenges their understanding of the world more strongly than they react to information that confirms their prior thinking. The concept of mental models and an understanding of confirmation bias help explain this reaction.

Mental models are the simplified understanding of the world that everyone carries within their heads. Our brains use these models to explain why certain causes generate certain effects and to predict what is likely to happen in the future.

As discussed in chapter 6, confirmation bias is our tendency to disregard evidence that challenges our existing beliefs and our inclination to favor evidence that supports those beliefs. In concert with mental models, it leads people to focus on information that reinforces their existing mental models and discount information that challenges them. Differing mental models and confirmation bias help explain why two individuals can receive the exact same information but still come to different conclusions about what it means.

---

[2] For an overview of the state of uncertainty research, listen to the interview with Jessica Hullman and Matthew Kay on the Data Stories podcast and consult the resources listed in the show notes. Yes, it's a podcast entirely about pictures. It's great. Enrico Bertini and Moritz Stefaner, hosts, "Visualizing Uncertainty with Jessica Hullman and Matthew Kay," *DataStories* (podcast), January 19, 2019, https://datastori.es/134-visualizing-uncertainty-with-jessica-hullman-and-matthew-kay/.

As a result, people are far more resistant to conclusions that conflict with their existing mental models. These conclusions don't just add information to an audience's knowledge base. They require people to change their mental models of how the world works—a high bar to clear even without the pressure of confirmation bias. Expect your audience to challenge you much more heavily when your findings conflict with their mental models than when they conform to them.

Resistance can be anticipated with the Audience Confusion Matrix

The Audience Confusion Matrix combines the audience's perception of change and their prior expectations into a 2×2 matrix. With this model, you can predict how the audience will challenge you and prepare more effectively for those challenges. It's named after the confusion matrix—an analytical tool used in machine learning—because both compare expectations and reality in a 2×2 matrix.[3]

The Audience Confusion Matrix combines the answers to two questions
1. Does this audience expect a change—in ratio—of some underlying phenomenon?
2. Does this analysis observe a change—in ratio—of some underlying phenomenon?

Each quadrant of the Audience Confusion Matrix describes a different combination of data expectation and observation. The section that follows goes through the likely audience response to each scenario, from most accepting to most resistant, and then describes the preparation required for each.

---

[3] The confusion matrixes found in machine learning typically evaluate the performance of classification algorithms, which sort observations into predetermined categories. An algorithm that determines whether a picture depicts a dog or not is a classification algorithm. A confusion matrix compares the algorithm's predicted classification with the correct classification. The matrix displays the results in four quadrants: true positives, true negatives, false positives, and false negatives. It's called a confusion matrix because it allows the analyst to evaluate if the model is "confusing" categories by misidentifying them.

Audience expectation

	No change (in ratio)	Change (in ratio)
No change (in ratio)	**What's next?** **No conflict:** No change expected No change observed	**What did you miss?** **Conflict:** Change expected No change observed
Change (in ratio)	**What just happened?** **Conflict:** No change expected Change observed	**What do we do now?** **No conflict:** Change expected Change observed

Data observation

Developed by Robin Ganek & Miro Kazakoff

1. What's next? (no change expected, no change observed)

This is the situation where no one expects anything to change and nothing changes. Expect little resistance in this scenario, because there is no conflict between the audience's expectation and the observed data. Often these situations are neither noticed nor discussed. When you review a dashboard in which all the metrics have remained consistent, you are in this scenario. These situations are simple and straightforward. The audience's goal is to move on to what's next on the agenda as quickly as possible.

Should you need to present this type of result, don't overcomplicate your communication. Be succinct. Consider if this is one of those situations where time spent meeting about the results could be replaced by an email. Focus almost entirely on next steps or implications for future action.

Examples of "what's next?" situations
- "3% of users logged a complaint last week. Our company policy is to keep this number below 4%."
- "The production server is still down. Like they said thirty minutes ago, the team is working on it and won't have another update until 2 p.m."

- "We invited another 1,000 people to our private beta test this month. As has been the case for the past eight months, about 40% signed up in the first week."
- "We ran our semiannual test to see if we need to recalibrate our production equipment. No major adjustments were needed."

Audience expectation

	No change (in ratio)	Change (in ratio)
No change (in ratio)	**What's next?** *We did the same things* *We got the same results* **No conflict:** No change expected No change observed	
Change (in ratio)		

(Left axis label: Data observation)

You should prepare for . . .

The audience to ask very few questions about the issue. If the topic is worthy of any discussion, the audience is most likely to ask about next steps or implications for future actions. Some may ask about data sources or methodology as a form of due diligence.

You should avoid . . .

Preparing too much detail or talking for too long. Audiences can interpret lengthy explanations of simple situations as a signal that the situation is more complicated than it appears. It can provoke unnecessary and unproductive scrutiny. Even if the analysis took a long time and a lot of work, focus on confirming the audience's expectation that nothing has changed, and move on.

2. What do we do now? (change expected, change observed)

In this scenario, the audience expects a change to happen, and it does. Audiences are more engaged here than in the "what's next" scenario but less antagonistic than they tend to be in the next two scenarios. Correctly anticipating change before it happens is a rare sign of an effective organization. It requires keen insight into the future. Even when the change is negative, audiences can be somewhat consoled by the fact that they saw it coming.

In these scenarios, frame the discussion around the future. Let the audience decide whether they want to focus on the data or move right into the action plan.

Examples of "what do we do now?" situations

- "We built excess production capacity around the globe to minimize the impact of supply chain disruptions. Because of the global pandemic, the government has closed the borders around one of our major manufacturing centers."
- "Hadassah just delivered her baby. Everyone is healthy. You'll be in charge of executing the coverage plan while she's on maternity leave."
- "On move-in day, roughly 30,000 cars will enter and exit campus. That's ten times our normal daily traffic."

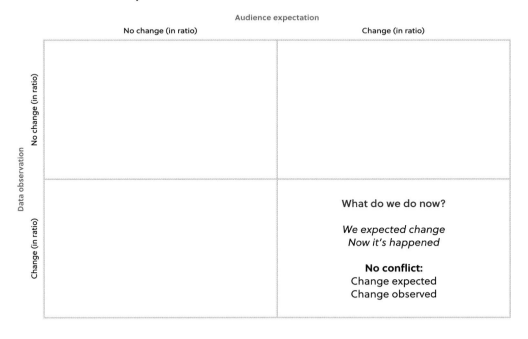

You should prepare for . . .

The audience to move immediately to a discussion of next steps if the change is positive. Think through the concrete actions required to manage the change, and focus on the data that informs the decisions the audience needs to make. Be ready to provide data on demand in response to specific elements of the action plan rather than all at once up front.

If the audience is nervous, take a moment to remind everyone that this change was expected. If the change is positive, prepare a plan that takes advantage of this unique moment.

You should avoid . . .

Spending extensive time on the data if the audience is ready to move to actions.

3. What just happened? (no change expected, change observed)

Sometimes unexpected changes happen. In these situations, something changes that the audience was not expecting to change. This is the first scenario discussed where expectation and reality conflict. Expect this conflict to generate a higher level of resistance from the audience.

Move quickly in this scenario. The dominant audience response to the "what just happened?" scenario is uncertainty. Even when the change is positive, the surprise can rattle people. Seek to understand what happened in as much detail as possible as quickly as possible. Split your time with the audience between explaining what happened and discussing the next steps that take advantage of the change or mitigate its damage.

Examples of "what just happened?" situations
- "A popular Instagrammer just posted a video raving about how great our product is. The video has already been seen over 100 million times."
- "The worst snowstorm in decades just caved in the roof of our primary facility. Thankfully no one was hurt, but the building is destroyed."
- "Our biggest prospect just asked us to submit a proposal for their business even though it's only been six months since they renewed their contract with our competitor."

	No change (in ratio)	Change (in ratio)
No change (in ratio)		
Change (in ratio)	**What just happened?** *We did the same thing* *Something different happened* **Conflict:** No change expected Change observed	

(Left axis label: Data observation)

You should prepare for . . .

The audience to want to take action. There may be strong disagreement about what that action ought to be.

Bring the audience a plan with next steps. Even if the plan is rough, it can help focus the audience's thinking. It's easier for the audience to react to any plan—even if it is deeply flawed—than it is for them to create one from scratch.

Focus on explaining what happened, but be ready to explain what action the data implies the organization ought to take. Since these changes are usually the result of an external shock rather than an internal action, audiences don't look to assign blame as readily as they do in the next scenario. Inaction is harder to find fault with than action, unless the inaction represents an oversight. Still, you should be prepared to answer questions about why the organization failed to anticipate this change and how to better prepare for similar situations in the future.

You should avoid . . .

Jumping right into the analysis. Take the audience's side. Empathize with whatever they are feeling—positive or negative—to help them process the surprise before going into the data.

4. What did you miss? (change expected, no change observed)

In this scenario, the audience expects a change, usually as a result of some action, that fails to materialize. In the most common version of this scenario, someone takes an action designed to create change and that action fails to generate any significant impact. Since actions require time and/or money, this is the scenario where an audience discovers those resources were wasted, and that their mental model of cause and effect is broken.

The profound discomfort generated by that discovery tends to make this the most challenging of the four scenarios. It is the scenario that suggests both that the audience's understanding of the world is flawed and that they are powerless to change it.

Often, audiences focus their discomfort with these results on the communicator. The audience may interpret the data with an intent—conscious or not—to assign or avoid blame.

Spend the most time preparing for this scenario. Be ready to explain the source of the data and the analytical process in a high degree of detail. If you cannot explain why the change the audience expected failed to occur, come ready with a plan to gather the data that will explain the discrepancy.

Examples of "what did you miss?" situations

- "We ran a month-long experiment to compare a 30-day free trial offer with a 14-day free trial offer. We expected the 30-day free trial to perform better. There was no statistically significant difference between the two: 5% of the 30-day group and 5% of the 14-day group purchased a subscription."
- "The marketing budget for the West increased 30% more than every other region in the country last year, by nearly $45 million, but sales in every region grew at the same rate."
- "Over the last twenty years we have recruited roughly equal numbers of male and female entry-level managers, but 85% of the people promoted to senior management are male."
- "You said we would get a break during the summer as people went on vacation, but we are as busy as ever."

	No change (in ratio)	Change (in ratio)
No change (in ratio)		What did you miss? *We did something new* *Nothing changed* **Conflict:** Change expected No change observed
Change (in ratio)		

Data observation

You should prepare for . . .

The audience to challenge the data, the analysis, and the decision-making. Expect the audience to ask lots of questions that begin with "Did you consider . . ." and strongly imply that you ought to have done so.

Remind the audience about what was known when the decisions were made and the reasoning at the time. If this was a test or a pilot, repeatedly remind them that this is the purpose of tests, and that even though no change was observed, that does not mean nothing was learned. Discuss what was learned, even if it was not intended learning.

Acknowledge emotion and remind the audience that you are disappointed and surprised too. Bring them a plan to gather the information that will help explain the discrepancy between what they expected and what happened.

You should avoid . . .

Obfuscating the results or becoming defensive when challenged. The audience will want an immediate explanation that helps explain how an action could fail to generate a reaction. The easiest explanation is that someone else made a mistake.

Avoid speculation while the audience is still focused on assigning blame. Speculation during this period focuses an audience on evaluating your thought process rather than the importance of gathering the information that will help the organization learn from this experience. Focus the audience on the soundness of your plan to gather that information, and explain how this new information will address their confusion.

Don't underestimate how frustrating this situation is for the audience. Since you have had more time to understand and accept the findings, you may forget the frustration and confusion you probably experienced when you initially reviewed them. Remember that your audience is experiencing a similar range of emotions.

WATCH OUT: Expectations change quickly

Since the audience's reaction depends on their expectations, their reactions change as fast as their expectations change. The news that a marketing campaign failed to work may be unexpected the first time an audience sees the results but may turn into an expected result by the end of the same meeting. The Curse of Knowledge can wipe the audience's memory of their own expectations with shocking speed. Prepare for audiences to move quickly from surprise to the belief that "I knew that was never going to work."

WATCH OUT: Magnitude and directionality matter

Frameworks, like all mental models, simplify reality to help clarify it. The Audience Confusion Matrix reduces the audience's response and the data into binary choices between change and no change. In reality, the magnitude and direction of the change will influence the intensity of the audience's response.

Rarely does the data show no change at all. Random variation alone will cause some change in the data. Your audience's response will be proportional to the magnitude of the change. If you increased headcount by 20%, a 10% increase in output won't provoke the same level of concern as a 0% change in output, even if both signal that the investment failed to generate a proportional change.

Similarly, the direction of the change will influence audience response. When a measure that the audience expects to get worse stays the same, the audience is likely to be relieved even though the decision-making failure and the opportunity to learn from it are no less significant than they would be if the situation had been reversed. This speaks to the power and importance of setting expectations. As you develop more nuanced expertise, expect your mental model of the Audience Confusion Matrix to become more complex by incorporating these additional dimensions.

Use the Audience Confusion Matrix to make your communication plan

Communication is an ongoing process. Assuming you'll review your analysis during a meeting, use the Audience Confusion Matrix to think about how you will prepare others before the meeting, frame the communication during the meeting, present the findings, and explain what comes next.

		Prepare others	Frame the communication	Present the findings	Explain next steps
What's next?		Unneeded	"This may be a short meeting."	Be brief and clear.	Introduce plans for the future or discuss risks only if appropriate.
	What do we do now?	Get buy-in on next steps if there is no clear action plan for this expected change.	"This was something we thought could happen. I want to focus on what we do now. I can walk through the data at whatever level you want."	Plan to move quickly from data to next steps, unless the change is the opposite of what was expected.	Present a plan to react to the expected change.
What just happened?		Get key stakeholders comfortable with the next steps. Discuss data at a high level.	"This was not something any of us expected. I'm also [surprised/ excited/ disappointed/ worried]."	Split time between data review and next steps. Take enough time to review what has changed. Focus on explaining causes and effects.	Present a plan for actions to capitalize on or mitigate the change. Focus the discussion around actions.
	What did you miss?	Get key stakeholders comfortable with the data. Discuss the conclusions and offer time for additional reviews after incorporating their feedback.	"I'm disappointed/ surprised too. I'm sure you have lots of questions. We will discuss the data in detail and then talk about next steps."	Spend most of the time reviewing the data. Remind everyone what info you had then and what info you have now.	Present a plan to gather more info. Focus the discussion on what information would explain the results and what resources will be needed to gather that info.

Developed by Allen Telio

Resistance can be defused

Challenges present a unique opportunity to build credibility with the audience. Demonstrating an ability to understand and address the needs of the audience in the moment suggests a thoughtfulness that increases the credibility of your analysis. The primary predictor of your ability to respond well in the moment is the quality of your preparation. No strategy for handling an audience can substitute for good preparation and a deep understanding of your analysis. Ask yourself—or a colleague—what questions the audience is likely to have. Be ready to answer every question you can and should know the answer to. Your ability to know which questions you ought to be able to answer—and have that answer—is a critical factor in the audience's evaluation of your analysis.

While the content of your response may be the most important factor in the audience's reaction, it is not the only factor. The human tendency to substitute emotional assessments for rational ones—as discussed in chapter 7—means audiences may interpret discomfort you feel under pressure from them as a sign of your discomfort with the quality of your work. Help the audience focus on the data by projecting a confidence you may or may not feel.

When it feels like your audience has moved from questioning the data to challenging you, take a deep breath and try to use the strategies below to shift the focus back to the data.

Don't get defensive (ever)

Humans get defensive when we feel like we are under attack. Avoiding defensiveness requires you to put aside the strong signals from your mind and body that the audience's questions represent a threat. Start with the assumption that the audience members have good intentions and just want clarity, even when their tone suggests otherwise. The more you behave like this is true, the more the audience will too.

Still, even when the audience doesn't intend to attack you, the internal signals that something is wrong can be overwhelming. Try to notice and break down the components of your physical experience from one of all-consuming terror to a combination of discrete physical experiences. Sweating, elevated heart rate, rapid shallow breathing, tremors, and even nausea are common responses.

You can mentally reframe these signals. Remind yourself that signals of anxiety from your body are normal. They do not signal anything about how the audience feels. All they signal is that you care about your work and the audience's opinion of it. These forms of stress response are your body's normal reaction to situations where the outcome matters. Like the similar feelings most experience before a big game or a performance, tell yourself that these physical signs are your body's way of preparing you to perform.

Acknowledge the audience's emotions

When faced with a hostile challenge, bring the audience back to the facts by naming and acknowledging the emotion behind the comment. Starting a response by saying "I understand that the lack of clarity is upsetting" or "I hear how angry you are about this" allows you to acknowledge feelings that were unsaid and transition to a less emotional and less personal explanation of why this issue might be unclear. For this to work you have to correctly identify and name the underlying emotion. Don't let that hurdle dissuade you from this technique. Learning how to do this well is a skill that requires practice.

Align yourself with the audience when emotions are mutual. If the findings surprise or disappoint them, share that you had the same reaction. Avoid sharing emotions that are in conflict with the audience's emotions, such as any frustration you might feel with their questions.

Remind the audience of what they knew back then

The Curse of Knowledge fuels many challenging questions. Knowing what we know now, past decisions can look transparently foolish. Audiences will want to know which group of idiots made such dumb choices. The idiots they seek to blame—of course—are often themselves. Audiences attempting to reconcile the frustration of an uncertain and changing world often ask communicators to do the impossible: predict the future, guarantee against uncertainty, and find signal where there is only noise.

Assume that no one remembers any mental state prior to the one they hold right now, and that they forget that all past decisions were made by people without the information we know now. Remind people what information was known at the time as often as necessary, and explain how past decisions emerged from that context. When the audience is focused on the data—rather than on your decision-making process as in the "what did you miss?" scenario—you may speculate about the future implications of the data, but be clear about what is certain and what is uncertain, what is knowable and what is unknowable.[4]

Don't excuse past poor judgement. Focus instead on how the new data changes our understanding so that we can make better decisions in the future. If you prepare well and know what you should know, audiences will—grudgingly—accept that there are things that are unreasonable to have known back then, things that remain unknown now, and things that will be impossible to ever know.

---

[4] Consider starting answers with a reminder that, "No one can predict the future, but I think the data suggests …"

Explain whether a change in the data would change the decision

The purpose of data in a business context is to drive better decisions. Defuse challenges that undermine your analysis by refocusing the audience on the decisions they need to make. Show them how far off an input or assumption would need to be in order to change that decision. You will find that most inputs can tolerate a large margin of error before they change the decision that the data addresses.

For example, imagine you have analyzed the total cost to install and operate four different customer relationship management (CRM) software packages. The goal is to decide which vendors should be invited in for a demonstration based on the total cost to purchase and operate their software. If someone challenged your assumption about the support costs of the cheapest option, you could explain how large the change in support costs would need to be before it reordered the ranking. If a 10× change in support costs wouldn't change the cost ranking, the audience would probably agree that improving the accuracy of this assumption is not worth the research time required to generate a more precise estimate.

Different standards apply to different decisions. If your analysis suggested that more staff were needed for each CRM's internal support team, the audience might need a high level of precision around support costs because they impact staffing. Assumptions that significantly change how many people a manager needs to hire—or fire—demand more accuracy. The difference is the decision that the data affects.

To do this, you must understand how all your analyses connect to the decisions the audience needs to make. This is a high standard, but also a best practice that will help you focus your communications on the all-important answer to the question of What's In It For Them—the WIIFT.

Fielding these challenges in real time requires you to understand your analysis, present your findings in a clear, logical structure, and sometimes perform quick mental math. These conversations will defuse most challenges, but they will also reveal areas where additional work is warranted. Demonstrate wisdom to your audience by committing to justifiable extra work as vigorously as you defend your analysis from challenges that don't change the outcome.

Getting good at this kind of real-time sensitivity testing requires considerable practice and mental clarity, but it results in a powerful skill. The ability to understand which inputs matter to a decision is a critical skill for leaders in any domain. Recognizing what matters both speeds up decision-making and focuses you on the most important problems. That speed and impact compound quickly over all the decisions leaders have to make.

Key concepts from this chapter

Don't mistake low resistance from an audience for high acceptance of your conclusions. Resistance is a unique opportunity to capitalize on audience engagement to increase your credibility and strengthen support for your analysis.

THE DEFUSING RESISTANCE CHECKLIST

Have you	Test your audience response plan
Identified a meaningful change?	• Have you converted all values into ratios to see there has been a meaningful change?
Identified the audience's expectations?	• Have you asked someone in your potential audience what they expect to happen?
Identified which quadrant of the Audience Confusion Matrix you are in?	• Have you prepared the audience (if needed)? • Have you decided how to frame the conversation? • Have you presented your analysis at the appropriate level of detail? • Have you generated appropriate next steps?
Identified the questions your audience is likely to ask you and your likely response?	• Do you know the answers to all the questions you should be expected to know the answer to? • Have you considered the likely emotional state of your audience? • Can you recognize your body's signals that you are getting defensive so you can manage them? • Are you clear about what was known when this decision was made or this analysis was performed? • Do you understand the decisions your audience needs to make so that you can identify what impacts those decisions?

If you remember nothing else . . .

Resistance shows that the audience cares. It is one of the few ways you can know for certain that your audience is engaged.

No strategy for handling an audience can substitute for good preparation and a deep understanding of your analysis.

Start with the assumption that the audience has good intentions and just wants clarity, even when their tone suggests otherwise.

Exercise: What type of scenario is it?

You have found yourself in the situations below and need to share your thoughts in a meeting with your company's senior leadership team. You prepared your boss with your thoughts but have not had time to connect with anyone else in the meeting. You assume it's the first time everyone other than your boss will learn about this. For each situation:

1. **Identify which of the four scenarios best describes this situation.** Use the scenario to inform your response.
2. **Write out how you want to frame the discussion.**
3. **Propose next steps.** Assume that senior management expects next steps to accompany anything that reaches their level, but that the purpose of these next steps is to jump-start a discussion. The proposed next steps do not have to be perfect, they just have to help senior management think about the actions they might take.

What's the situation?

Our two largest competitors just surprised the industry with a merger announcement. Almost all of our customers are also customers of at least one of the two competitors. Both companies have a large suite of products, some of which overlap our offering, but many of which do not. They have announced that they will merge sales forces and administrative staff.

What type of scenario is it?

Audience expectation

	No change (in ratio)	Change (in ratio)
No change (in ratio)	**What's next?** No change expected No change observed	**What did you miss?** Change expected No change observed
Change (in ratio)	**What just happened?** No change expected Change observed ✗	**What do we do now?** Change expected Change observed

Data observation (left axis label)

The speed of the merger means it's likely an unexpected change.

A well-executed merger changes the new org's ability to compete with us.

Note the reasons why you identified this scenario.

How would you frame the discussion?

"This merger caught all of us by surprise. It's concerning that the merged organization will have relationships with almost all of our customers and a broader product suite, but we still don't know much about their plans.

"Today, I'll go through all of our customers that are already customers of either company and identify which ones we think are most at risk for us as a result of this merger."

What next steps would you propose?

- Brief the sales team on the situation.
- Create answers to questions customers are likely to have.
- Meet with the most at-risk customers to assess the risk and learn what the new competitor is saying to them.
- Create a framework and process to pool the information from these customer meetings.
- Set up a future meeting to review new information and adjust the plan.

Think through how you would frame the discussion with others and propose next steps.

What's the situation?

A new nationwide marketing program drove $496K in sales to your website with a spend of $100K. A pilot version of this campaign drove $25K in sales with a spend of $5K last quarter.

What type of scenario is it?

Audience expectation

	No change (in ratio)	Change (in ratio)
No change (in ratio)	What's next? No change expected No change observed	What did you miss? Change expected No change observed
Change (in ratio)	What just happened? No change expected Change observed	What do we do now? Change expected Change observed

Data observation (left axis label)

How would you frame the discussion?

What next steps would you propose?

What's the situation?

Last year your company hired three people from your university with no direct recruiting efforts or spending. For the first time this year, your company began a major on-campus recruiting initiative via the school's career office. The effort cost nearly 10% of the recruiting team's annual budget. It resulted in four new hires.

What type of scenario is it?

	Audience expectation	
	No change (in ratio)	Change (in ratio)
No change (in ratio) (Data observation)	What's next? No change expected No change observed	What did you miss? Change expected No change observed
Change (in ratio) (Data observation)	What just happened? No change expected Change observed	What do we do now? Change expected Change observed

How would you frame the discussion?

What next steps would you propose?

What's the situation?

You sell software to help interest groups track state legislation and lobby more effectively. As expected, a single party just won the House, Senate, and Governorship in your biggest state market. When a single party controls all three, significantly more legislation is passed.

What type of scenario is it?

Audience expectation

	No change (in ratio)	Change (in ratio)
No change (in ratio)	**What's next?** No change expected No change observed	**What did you miss?** Change expected No change observed
Change (in ratio)	**What just happened?** No change expected Change observed	**What do we do now?** Change expected Change observed

Data observation

How would you frame the discussion?

What next steps would you propose?

What's the situation?

Your team has been predicting that new market entrants will increase the demand for mauxite—a critical raw material for your product—and drive up its price. Based on your analysis, the company has been spending heavily to stockpile mauxite. Through unrelated mismanagement, two new market entrants went bankrupt, and the price of mauxite has declined sharply. It's now not expected to recover for years.

What type of scenario is it?

Audience expectation

	No change (in ratio)	Change (in ratio)
No change (in ratio)	**What's next?** No change expected No change observed	**What did you miss?** Change expected No change observed
Change (in ratio)	**What just happened?** No change expected Change observed	**What do we do now?** Change expected Change observed

Data observation

How would you frame the discussion?

What next steps would you propose?

Acknowledgments

In the practical sense, what you've just read is a textbook, but what I've just written feels in part like a memoir. Every idea in this book was something that I learned. The people thanked here were there for many of those moments. I've learned with and from all of them. I could not be more thankful for how they continue to help me make sense of the world.

Like everyone, I stand firmly on the shoulders of others. This book owes a great debt to the thinking and work of so many, but especially Nancy Duarte, Stephen Few, Barbara Minto, Mary Munter, and Cole Nussbaumer-Knaflic.

My students at MIT Sloan inspire me and give meaning to my workdays. They have shaped the exercises and presentation of this material as much as I have. Thank you Hugues Coruzzi, Meital Haas, Nicholas Judson, Jennifer Lien, Roxanne Moslehi, Ananya Mukkavilli, Molly Spector, Nicole Stutz, and Sohpia Xing for being my TAs and sounding boards. Special thanks to Radhika Brinkopf and Faye Cheng, who TA'd the first versions of the class from which this material emerged.

I'm supported by a team of people both personally and professionally. Thank you Dylan Girard, Prita Manganiello, Noelle McClanahan, Joe Riley, and all the folks at Cannytrophic Design for keeping my mind, body, soul, and calendar functioning. Thanks to Ted Gup and Hannah England who provided housing at various points. You made my romantic visions of writing a book deep in the Maine woods come true.

Thank you to the design and editorial team, who should be considered co-authors of this book. Judith Feldmann, Candace Hope, Katie Kashkett, Elizabeth Moran, and Emily Taber are the best in the business.

To learn from the world-class teachers I work with is a daily gift. Thank you Nina Birger, Kara Blackburn, Lori Breslow, Chris Cullen, Neal Hartman, Virginia Healy-Tangney,

Arathi Mehrotra, Roberta Pittore, Melissa Webster, and JoAnne Yates. Thank you Ben Shields for teaching me how to structure a class and co-teaching the first version of Communicating with Data with me. Alan Telio, your insights have refined the class, this text, and my approach to my career—thank you. Christine Kelly, without you I would not have this job nor the gift of your friendship. Just one of those blessings would have been enough.

Alex, Andy, Bobby, Jim, John, Matt, and Will—the boys and girl; now men, women, and children of R St.—I became an adult with you. Chase, John, Mike, and Stephen, you were there even before that. I'm so grateful you've stuck around to see how it all turned out.

To Elizabeth, who convinced me to take that teaching job; Melissa, without whom this book would not have begun; and Renée, without whom it would not have been finished—thank you.

To those who read various parts of this book, it is immeasurably better for your input. Thank you Arathi Mehrotra, Barbara Minto, Mary Munter, Michael Newman, Pilar Opazo, Jack Sullivan, and Ann Forest West.

Tom Rose, you have been my business and thought partner for over a decade. I don't remember whose ideas are whose anymore. I'm glad to not even have to care.

Noah Freeman, you helped hone the ideas in here over two decades of friendship, read every word in the manuscript, and then reordered half of them. I'm typing this sentence in the condo you let me borrow. You are a truly great friend.

And finally, to my parents who gave me life and my entire family who sustain it. JJ and Andrew, you brought Stacey, Becca, Ezra, Zoe, Abie, Asher, Zac, and Hadassah into my life. This book is dedicated to you. With you, the future looks brighter than the past.

to JJ & Andrew
my brothers by birth,
my family by choice

For more information and resources, visit
www.PersuadingWithData.com

Bibliography

Anscombe, F. J. "Graphs in Statistical Analysis." *American Statistician* 27 (Feb 1973): 17–21.

Ariely, Daniel. *Predictably Irrational*. Harper, 2009.

Berinato, Scott. *Good Charts: The HBR Guide to Making Smarter, More Persuasive Data Visualizations*. Harvard Business Review Press, 2016.

Cairo, Alberto. *The Truthful Art: Data, Charts, and Maps for Communication*. New Riders, 2016.

Cialdini, Robert. *Influence: The Psychology of Persuasion*. Rev. ed. Harper Business, 2006.

"Conceptual Parallelism." Sloan Communication Program Teaching Note. Unpublished teaching note. N.d.

Corbett, Edward P. J., and Robert J. Connors. *Classical Rhetoric for the Modern Student*. 4th ed. Oxford University Press, 1999.

Duarte, Nancy. *DataStory: Explain Data and Inspire Action Through Story*. O'Reilly Media, 2019.

Duarte, Nancy. *Slide:ology: The Art and Science of Creating Great Presentations*. O'Reilly Media, 2008.

Evergreen, Stephanie D. H. *Effective Data Visualization: The Right Chart for the Right Data*. Sage Publications, 2017.

Few, Stephen. *Now You See It: Simple Visualization Techniques for Quantitative Analysis*. Analytics Press, 2009.

Few, Stephen. *Show Me the Numbers: Designing Tables and Graphs to Enlighten*. 2nd ed. Analytics Press, 2012.

French, J. R. P., Jr., and B. Raven. "The Bases of Social Power." In *Studies in Social Power*, edited by Dorwin Cartright, 150–167. Institute for Social Research, 1959.

Heath, Chip, and Dan Heath. *Made to Stick: Why Some Ideas Survive and Others Die*. Random House, 2007.

Kahneman, Daniel. *Thinking, Fast and Slow.* Farrar, Straus and Giroux, 2015.

Kazakoff, Miro, and Robin Ganek. "The Audience Confusion Matrix." Lecture, Massachusetts Institute of Technology Course 15.276: Communicating with Data. Spring 2017.

Knaflic, Cole Nussbaumer. *Storytelling with Data: A Data Visualization Guide for Business Professionals.* John Wiley & Sons, 2015.

Kosara, Robert. "An Illustrated Tour of the Pie Chart Study Results." Accessed August 11, 2020. https://eagereyes.org/blog/2016/an-illustrated-tour-of-the-pie-chart-study-results.

Kotter, John P. *Power and Influence: Beyond Formal Authority.* Free Press, 1985.

Minto, Barbara. *The Pyramid Principle: Logic in Writing and Thinking.* 3rd ed. Financial Times Prentice Hall, 2010.

Munter, Mary, and Lynn Hamilton. *Guide to Managerial Communication: Effective Business Writing and Speaking.* 10th ed. Pearson, 2014.

Patterson, Kerry. *Crucial Conversations: Tools for Talking When Stakes Are High.* 2nd ed. McGraw-Hill, 2012.

Petty, R. E., and J. T. Cacioppo. "The Elaboration Likelihood Model of Persuasion." In *Communication and Persuasion.* Springer Series in Social Psychology. Springer, 1986.

Russell, Lynn, and Mary Munter. *Guide to Presentations.* 4th ed. Pearson, 2014.

Shah, A. K., and D. M. Oppenheimer. "Heuristics Made Easy: An Effort-Reduction Framework." *Psychological Bulletin* 134, no. 2 (2008): 207–222.

Thaler, Richard, and Cass Sunstein. *Nudge.* Penguin Books, 2009.

Tufte, Edward R. *Beautiful Evidence.* Graphics Press, 2006.

Tufte, Edward R. *Envisioning Information.* Graphics Press, 1991.

Tufte, Edward R. *The Visual Display of Quantitative Information.* 2nd ed. Graphics Press, 2001.

Tufte, Edward R. *Visual Explanations: Images and Quantities, Evidence and Narrative.* Graphics Press, 2007.

Ware, Colin. *Information Visualization: Perception for Design.* Elsevier, 2004.

Wexler, Steve, Jeffrey Shaffer, and Andy Cotgreave. *The Big Book of Dashboards: Visualizing Your Data Using Real-World Business Scenarios.* John Wiley & Sons, 2017.

Yates, JoAnne et al. "Craigstone Corporation Case." Unpublished case study, Massachusetts Institute of Technology Course 15.280: Communication for Leaders. N.d.

Zelazny, Gene. *Say It with Charts: The Executive's Guide to Successful Presentations.* 4th ed. McGraw-Hill, 2001.

Zelazny, Gene. *Say It with Presentations: How to Design and Deliver Successful Business Presentations.* Rev. ed. McGraw-Hill, 2006.

Index